ADVENTURES
OF RATEGAN

VOLUME 1

Dear David
Always
Snch a joy

R

ROBIN BENGER

The Adventures of Rategan: Volume 1
Copyright © 2023 by Robin Benger

Tellwell Talent
www.tellwell.ca

ISBN
978-0-2288-9366-0 (Paperback)
978-0-2288-9367-7 (eBook)

TABLE OF CONTENTS

INTRODUCTION

It was ten o clock at night by the time I touched down in Toronto.

I'd been away for three weeks, covering the US invasion of Grenada.

As was my custom I headed straight downtown to the Epicure.

Graham Greene and Jim Garrard were there.

"Hey. Whats up?"

"Grenada."

"You were there?"

"Just got in."

It was to these actors I would decompress.

The documentary I had made had already been broadcast.

My "official" story was out there, the primary assignment.

But always there was another narrative.

My personal story. What I had seen and absorbed. Something more profane, more dangerous, more from the heart.

And this was the story I spilled out into the bar on Queen Street West, belting back rum and coke until the rush kicked in.

Next day, I'd sleep in, stumble into the CBC "Sunday Morning" office, the old convent on Jarvis Street, and get my next assignment.

El Salvador, Libya, China or somewhere in North America where something exciting and historic was happening.

Many years after that, when I was 64, I went on a writing binge, throwing half a dozen stories against the wall.

Then I took three years off, and went and became a first class cricket umpire in North Yorkshire, and wrote a book about walking, a book of gentle adventures and reflections.

On my return to Canada in 2019, the pandemic.

Every morning I would lock myself into my Bunkie at the foot of the garden with my Mandela Flag and my cricket trophies and my thermos of rooibos tea, and write.

I was completely disinterested in writing about myself. Not even remotely famous enough for that.

So one day I invented a character. Rategan. Rategan, a racy, dashing name. Rategan Edwardes.

He would have all my adventures. With Rategan I could exaggerate and dramatise and compress. I was free to write.

These stories are quasi-literary versions of my Epicure debriefs to those actors on Queen Street West. The official documentaries can be found here and there, formal and structured.

I ended up with a thousand pages, 21 stories. Too much. It's cut down to six, here. There's another fifteen left for Volumes Two and Three.

I'd like to thank all the crews, and editors I worked with. They know who they are.

I'd like to acknowledge all the victims whose voices are unheard in the great anguished zones of the world.

And I salute my beloved wife Nicky who raised three incredible children...Griffin, Tess and Charlie...while I was larking about Hell's half-acre.

Cover design by Christopher Dew
Front Cover Photograph by Derek DeBono
Edited by Michael Winter and Andrew Forrest

1 RATEGAN DOES MOZAMBIQUE

APRIL 1980. MAPUTO, MOZAMBIQUE.

She opens the door to Rategan; bent over, hand on a child, looking up at him through brown hair, plastered on her sweaty forehead.

"Yes?"

Hot, bothered, fearful, strong, paranoid, beautiful, interrupted.

Thandi.

Across the continent, on the west side, also by the humid African sea. Lobango, Angola. Jeannette, a baby on her hip, bringing in the mail. There's a package, addressed to her husband. She puts her daughter down.

She opens the package.

At the detonation, across the city, people flinch. From a distance they can see the smoke puff out of a blown window as the echo rolls across the roofs and out to sea. Two images of two women in the frontline states. In the 1970s, in nations bordering on the northern edges of apartheid South Africa. He has met both women. In Thandi's case it's what he saw, in the other, Jeannette in Angola, it's a bombing he imagines. And the imagination is unlimited, even to the way the flesh was torn.

Rategan has another image. A bomber. It is some years later, after apartheid.

He is on all fours on the floor of his hardware shop.
Beneath him, a large rectangular piece of glass.
"Can I help you?" he says
"Are you Albie Botes?" Rategan says.
Botes regards the visitor.
What does he see?
A man as big as he is, longer hair, shoulder bag.
He turns back to his task. Skrrrit. The knife cuts along
the side of the glass. He taps it with the back of the tool.
Clink. It falls onto the day's newspapers. He turns back.
"Who wants to know?"
"My name is Rategan. I'm doing a documentary about
the death squads, for Canadian television."

The man on the floor glances at an elderly woman
fussing for something in the back of the shop.

"Ek sal môre daardie ding vir jou hê, Tannie"

She looks at him, gets the code between people who
have been surrounded by danger for generations, the
kaffirs, the English redcoats; and makes to leave.

Botes waits until she's gone, the door clanking shut,
chimes tinkling.
Methodically, he tidies up.
Sweeps up the cuttings into the newspaper and dumps
it in the trash.
Removes his gloves, unflustered.
Puts the glass cutter under the counter. Makes a note
in a little black leather book. Black biro. Flips it shut.
Peers out into the street, through the glass. Through the
sign Arniston Hardwinkel in an arc, red lettering.
The eyes turn to Rategan, attention now focused.
"How did you find me?"

"It's a long story".

TWENTY-FIVE YEARS EARLIER.
OCTOBER 13 1970.

Rategan is supposed to play cricket that Sunday. Not as in indulge in a silly game. As in, one of the top young players in the nation, playing at the highest level. With success, anxiety. The feeling that would always return. That something isn't right with all of this. South Africa. The muzzled majority, restless for its time. He has become fidgety, combative, wanting to do everything prohibited now that he is liberated from the straitjacket of a strict private school, a school which solves the problem of injustice by training its boys to shoot for the stratosphere, to that rare altitude where Money sits with God, protecting the guilty.

He has nailed the cricket bit, but seeks something more, something he must descend into, something that is ticking in the heart of apartheid. Once, when he climbs one of the highest peaks in the Drakensberg Mountains, he feels the irresistible urge to fling himself off the precipice of Giant's Castle. He feels indestructible, chosen to prevail in any conflict. He's read Paradise Lost at 17. Damn good at everything. Arrogant. Oblivious.

When, one day on campus, he sees a flyer pinned to a pole inviting anyone interested to join the University Christian Movement in a one-day seminar on apartheid and Christianity at faraway Turfloop University, a "black" university, he recognises a door he been looking to go through. A seminar on a black campus north of Pietersburg, five hours north, near the Rhodesian border.

Apartheid and Christianity. The heart of the issue. Not the Christianity of the white elites, of which he is a product.

When he tells his cricket captain the reason he can't play that weekend, another match they have to win, he says.

"You must be joking"

"No. I want to do this more."

The captain's cheeks flush red.

"You are out of your fucking mind. These people are communists, Rategan. Go off with them and and you'll end up sliced up in some township. You're putting your entire cricket career in jeopardy."

"I'll be back."

"We will see about that, not you."

Rategan shrugs, picks up his cricket bag and strolls away from the nets.

"Think about it, Rats. Think hard, man" the captain yells after him.

MAPUTO, MOZAMBIQUE

Thandi has opened the door to him, but it isn't her he's come to see. He has come to see Murray Levine, her partner. Rategan is in Mozambique on behalf of the Canadian Broadcasting Corporation, putting together a radio documentary on reports of a growing famine. Along with half a dozen foreign journalists, he is stuck in Maputo, waiting for a government approved plane to take them north to Inhambane, the famine zone.

It's an opportunity to make contact with a group of South Africans who fascinate him, and who he deeply admires. Some of his contemporaries from the time when he was expelled from South Africa have chosen to come here, to the so-called frontline states, to join the freedom fighters, join the struggle within striking distance of the assassins and jet bombers of apartheid. Ten years earlier, he had skipped all the way to Canada, to put all this insanity behind him, to start again. Then, he was resigned to the apparent truth that the bad guys had won, that apartheid had prevailed. Every opposition group was banned, their leaders imprisoned or in exile. Opposing apartheid, above or below ground, had become risky business.

He has been here in Maputo for a week, and desperately needs a Canadian to interview. For his audience, a Canadian pretty well has to be involved, either as a perpetrator, or in a Florence Nightingale role, or as a victim. He has been told of Levine, who has been there for a couple of years as a housing consultant for an aid group. Very articulate, knows the scene, he'd been told back in Toronto. Maybe not directly involved in the famine, but any Canuck in a drought. And he might know people up-country in the famine zone. Thandi, as it turns out, a South African, has recently moved in with him, with her infant daughter. She is a handsome woman who strikes him immediately as having enormous certitude, even though doubled over by the demands of this child and doubtless a host of financial and political worries. The father of the child is a prominent member of the ANC brains trust here, a key intellectual.

Rategan has come from the air-conditioned oasis of the Polana Hotel, half filled with apartheid spooks, Soviet bloc arm twisters, and those vulture capitalists of indeterminate nationality who thrive in failing African states like blue beetles on roadkill. In search of Levine, he has driven his green Datsun rental down Avenida Julius Nyerere, past the roundabout with the big red box cube with yellow Marxist slogans, into the parking lot of a four-storey apartment building, right on the seafront. As in seaside cities a few hundred miles away in the apartheid south, the wind blows beach sand into drifts over the car park. In Durban, black street sweepers earn a few rands sweeping it off so the white holidaymakers don't take sand into their cars, man. Here it piles up.

Levine, in radio documentary parlance, turns out to be a first class clipster, someone who speaks clearly, in short and effective insights. His eyes are lined with the weariness of the long-distance idealist. Wise beyond his years, a deeply earnest version of the comedian Eugene Levy. He describes a society crippled by constant crises, with mountains to climb before any Canadian tax dollars can do any good, particularly in the housing sector. Rategan remembers one thing he says. In Africa, 90 percent of the people have, at some point in their lives, slept in the open, without a roof over their heads or walls to protect them. In other words, out in the open, in the bush, or in abandoned city lots and buildings. Freedom, he says, has come to Mozambique in spirit only.

In the background Thandi makes haste to disappear, not wanting any attention. Her accent pegs her as one of Rategan's people, a white South African who loathes apartheid as well, and here doing a lot more about it than he is; and every second a target for Pretoria.

Back at the age of eighteen, the cricketing Rategan waits outside his parents' townhouse, waiting in the 5 am darkness for his pick-up car, knowing he is headed in absolutely the right "wrong" direction, the opposite direction from the cricket field. His inner Christian thirsts for this rare opportunity, meeting black South Africans on an equal basis. He'd always thought all the "happy" blacks he encountered, the servant class, are all lying with their spectacular smiles and beautiful songs and tireless, uncomplaining, grossly underpaid labour.

The rage he feels is deep and abiding. It has already separated him from his "circle", including his family. Like a soundless and irrevocable tectonic split. South Africa to him is one big sick dark joke, a massive case of deception, dishonesty and heavily-armed cruelty. You can see the rotted innards of the ruling class, the inner cancer that twists the oppressor, in the obliterating way young white men like him drink, fight, drive, get killed. It's a death wish.

The ride arrives and he squeezes into the back. The driver, a middle-aged man with Kennedy-like hair and an open shirt turns out to be a famous Catholic anti-apartheid cleric, Canon Bryce Steward. He drives fast with his arm resting on the window as they clear the suburban bungalows and shanty townships for the Highveld and the sun comes up and he and the woman in charge, also with an incredible mane of hair, are making jokes about Vorster and Herzog. There's the smell of freedom in the air.

Four hours later they are greeted by a line of black and Indian theology students, their body language immediately different. Instead of the broken and slumped bodies of the masses, the oppressed, there's self-esteem. Straight backs, easy swinging arms initiating handshakes and hugs and laughter. In his decade in South Africa it is an utterly unprecedented case of amity between people of colour and whites. To Rategan, it's a kind of miracle. He senses this day is changing his life.

He immediately gets that heart ignition of black self-confidence fired by equality, his equals at last, no smarter or dumber than he. But they are all older than him. These men and women already have degrees and are in their late twenties. A decade of apartheid propaganda about education curls up and slinks away forever from his soul, it's tail between its legs, shamed. Jeannette Curtis, the woman in the front seat, is the natural leader of their group. She knows them all, by their first names. They seem to love and respect her, hanging on her very word.

Inside a church hall there's tea in metal vat; chipped ceramic cups, hot on the knuckle. And sandwiches, with processed meat.

There's a typewritten page pinned up to a board with the day's agenda.

CHRISTIANITY AND APARTHEID:

9:30-10:30 Service. St Helen's.
Rev Ebenezer Mahlangu.
Apartheid.
What would Jesus Do?
Barney Pistorius - National President Young Christian League.
Father Bryce Steward - Director Kairos Center
Christy Halberstadt - University Christian Movement.

Session One:

Paths of Most Resistance

Jeannette Curtis: Nusas (Wits) V-P unions. And others.

He walks into the service full of anticipation, already raised up by a conversation he'd just had with a man who wore thick glasses and was a post-graduate student in theology, Thabo.

"So Rategan. What will you be saying about Christianity and apartheid?"

He looks around. What? First reaction. Did anyone hear that question? Tongue-tied. He remembers his mother telling him that now he will be in social situations with richer and more powerful people and in conversation he was never to talk about sex, religion or politics. Never.

"I dunno. What do you think?"

"Well." Thabo glances around and leans in, whispering in his ear.

"We are all here on government bursaries. Which means most of us are (snap)", he snaps his fingers in Rategan's face, and leans back.

"One phone call away from informing"

He is closer to Rategan's face in a way no black man has ever been.

"So we tend to keep our opinions to ourselves."

Rategan raises an eyebrow.

Thabo bursts into laughter.

"But not today, comrade. Today we talk freely, hey?"

He places his arm around his shoulders and leads him into the chapel.

Something big is about to happen in Rategan's life. He knows that he's so ready. Inside, he has been hoping for something like this for years.

There are about twenty-five of them in there. Half and Half.

They start. The first hymn. The voices are firm, harmonising effortlessly.

A white professor starts reading the first lesson.

Then.

BANG. The doors burst open to his right. Screams, a blur of khaki, a thunk and his arm seized, blue police caps.

The cops are closing down the service.

The men in blue swarm like furious wasps. Women scream, men yell. An officer announces.

"This is an illegal gathering. You are all under arrest"

Ten years later, at Eduardo Mondlane University in Mozambique, a man sits at his desk in an office beyond the bombed-out one.

He is a dark silhouette. Until he sees Rategan, waiting in an outer room with his bag with its tape recorder. He then stands up and leaves.

The light catches his expression as he glances back at Rategan. Hunted. Hostile.

Rategan has arrived at the Centre of African Studies for a prearranged interview with Rob Davies, an ANC ideologue who had gone to his university, Rhodes, back in SA, far across the border, beyond the green hills, fifteen hours drive south from here. The Centre of African Studies at Edouardo Mondlane University is the intellectual heart of the ANC in the frontline states. There's the island, where Mandela, Sisulu, Mbeki and the rest wait, counting the years.

London, where Tambo and Slovo scheme and plan.

And there's here, heads above the trenches, where Ruth First and the others live and work.

The day before, it's founding director and driving force, First, had been blown to smithereens by a parcel bomb. The windows of her office are still shattered, glass on the floor. There is still an orange stain of blood along the parquet floor.

Davies hollow-eyed, on automatic, gives Rategan an interview thick with Marxist jargon and irony, rock-hard beneath the trauma. There might have been lower points in their struggle, but this seems very low. The dark-haired man in the background, against the light of the dying afternoon, is Mark MacMahon. It is one of those names whispered along the radical telegraph. One of those white guys who has taken up arms with the black guys against the other white guys and their black guys.

He is also the father of that baby girl in Thandi's arms.

Rategan wonders about them. She, a Durban beauty with deep smarts, he, a man who could melt the heart out of any woman. In other circumstances they would have been the golden couple of their generation. They chose, together, to run, to disappear, go underground after their mentor, their professor is killed in Durban. A sweet, soft-spoken man with a flaming pen and an idea way too hot for the paranoid, half-literate thugs of the State[1]. One afternoon he answers the doorbell and a gunman's bullet hits him in the chest. The government denies any involvement. It's one in a series of such political assassinations. More than two thousand of them from that year, 1978, to when Mandela is released from prison 12 years later, in 1990. Twelve years. Killings, as the courts will deem, "by persons unknown". The message is, if we can't get you by law, we will now walk

---

[1] Rick Turner's "The Eye of The Needle" is a classic of South African political writing.

up your front path in broad daylight just when you are least expecting it, and, bang, in the name of the Republic. Mxenge, Webster, Lubowski, to name a few. Years later it all comes out. Many are done by government- backed undercover death squads. Even the tyre and petrol "necklace" killings at that time, blamed on "terrorists". (Terrorists trained, deployed and paid by the Botha/de Klerk governments.)

These were the days before the days of miracle and wonder, these "were the long-distance calls", to use Paul Simon's phrase.[2] Rategan is fascinated by the lives in the tunnel, the lives inside the ring. He watches them from afar hurtle from one exploding city to another -- he observing from a stationary position on a snowy, faraway bank, behind a desk in an office building, in Canada, with newspapers from around the world delivered to his desk daily.

And there she is at the door, in the heat, looking up through sweaty hair stuck to her forehead and cheek, trying to hold the squirming nappy on the squealing child, the other hand on the doorknob.
"Yes?" Like, what shit now??

She has come to Mozambique with one lover, a man firing the rhetoric of this historic revolution, like being tied to a boat being dragged by a demon. She has made her move. Taken the gap. Taken the huge gamble. Torn away from her Mother, Father and Brothers. She is a

---

2

young woman who stands very still. The dancer's body, the poise, the balance, the strong delicacy.

In Natal, in the inland coastal waters, the heron stands stock still on one leg, for hours.

Then she meets the man with the crystal brain, her professor, and then his student, the Irish flameboy, who has that particular combination of rage burned into ideology. And, in South Africa, the time has come, says Professor Crystal Brain. And here is the book. Here are the rules. This is the way and here, the masses surging at the gate. Your job? Unlock it.

Teach the rules to the masses, and see what rage-towards-injustice is unleashed. And this, all this you see about you, the cruelty, the arrogance, the brutality, the stupidity, the bovine submissiveness, the pathetic and awful reaching for taste and international acceptance, all this will be consumed by a righteous fire, a massive national wrong righted with words and codes and yes, with blasts and bombs, until all is settled and through the dust and the moans The Man walks out, into a cleansed future.

So Romeo and Juliet get into the bakkie with the false plates and turn north, to Mozambique and the killing fields of the struggle.

Someone mentions a party. The Colonel is going to be there. Rategan should meet the colonel. He is keen. He suspects that at the core of any nation or movement is an individual, a target for him. The Colonel, a Colonel in the Russian KGB, is a Lithuanian Jew who has risen through the ranks of law and revolution in post-war South Africa to be the most powerful military strategist in the leadership of the African National Congress.

After a shower at the Polana, and his third sighting of an enigmatic man in a white suit in his own corridor, who is he for Chrissakes, he gets to the place he was told the party is gathering.

He is asked to wait outside, on the street side of the fence, like a servant in the white suburbs of apartheid, while someone goes back in there to clear him.

While he waits, Rategan sees the shadows thrown by the fire against the trees and a house, some fifty yards off. There's music, Masekela, Ibrahim, Makeba. He thinks he sees Thandi there, in a soft cluster of shadows, long hair, long dress, moving to the music, earlier than the notes carried on the warm wind. Someone comes back,

"I'm sorry it's not OK. I don't know why. Things are weird. Sorry."

Fuck. Bad timing.

Some forks in the road you actually don't even get to, but can see, as close as 50 yards away. He looks over his shoulder. For a moment he thinks he glimpses a man with silver hair and glasses moving to the beat in the midst of people watching the fire. He remembers the Colonel likes to dance. He wonders why he is at a party so soon after his wife's horrific death.

Later he would learn that, earlier that day, the ANC representative in Zimbabwe has also been assassinated, machine-gunned, as he leaves his home in his car. The week before in Harare, Rategan had met the man. In response to Rategan's knock, Joe Gqabi had come to the door of his office above a furniture store in the Indian market area. Rategan had handed him an envelope someone in Canada had given him to deliver. The bearded man with off-kilter thick-framed glasses had looked nervous, had taken the envelope in a way that suggested to Rategan that he was avidly expecting whatever was inside, but disappointedly had said that he was too busy to meet him. Somebody had said Rategan had been there, and now here he was, here, where another assassination had happened, a parcel bomb for the Colonel's wife.

At the fence, Rategan stands for a while, toeing the red dust of Mozambique. Excluded.

"Shittt."

He hasn't earned the trust that opens these doors.

Now is the time.

Now's the time for the mid-expedition blow out.

Time to contact Jens, the tsetse fly guy. He'd flown in with a Dutchman who was clearly wild, who was running a European-funded tsetse fly eradication programme.

Jens had told Rategan that if he wanted to get wasted in Maputo, he was his man. Rategan follows the striding Jens, a towering fuck-you of a man, blond-haired and brown-bearded, shirt open, African patterned belt, rangy legs sticking out from his khaki shorts, big safari boots. Rategan follows as he weaves through the dripping beams of a half-finished high-rise office building somewhere in downtown Maputo.

They had gotten thoroughly plastered at the bar at the Polana, where Rategan tried to pick a fight with the white-suited guy who was always lurking in the corridor outside his room.

"Yer fucking jacket is way too corrupt".

This has pleased the man, who slithers closer, like a reptile attracted to slime.

"Allow me to introduce myself"

Hungarian? Spanish?

"Ari Ben-Yalla"

Israeli.

"Rategan Edwardes. Jens …"

"Van Toorn."

"Dutch."

"Uh-uh."

"You" (nodding at Rategan) "are English?"

The astute observer of things Africana will know that an Englishman in Africa is one of three things. A hopeless idealist. A well-mannered sadist. Or a mongrel.

"I'm a mongrel"

"And what brings you here, may I ask?"

"I'm doing a documentary for the Canadian Broadcasting Corporation"

"On what"

"Might be too dangerous to tell you"

"Try me."

"Arms dealers in Africa"

He pauses, taps on his glass. Looks around the bar. There's a black couple out of earshot, embracing.

"We might have some things to discuss"

"How about you?"

"I have some import interests. I have a base in Montreal. What are your plans, here?"

Rategan thinks any further time with this operator constitutes a major security risk.

"Well I think we are outta here," he says to Jens

As they leave, Yalla adds,

"You guys have no idea who I know. I may be of assistance."

"I may take you up on that."

Leave all doors open.

They are now in search of dagga[3]. On the way to the abandoned building downtown Rategan nearly rolls the green Datsun around the red block Marxist roundabout on Avenida Eduardo Mondlane, laughing at the idea, as he fishtails westwards, of dying in a midnight rush for drugs.

"I'd like to end it all in Mozambique,
Where all the girls are dancing cheek-to-cheek"[4]

---

[3] Marijuana

[4] Bob Dylan "Mozambique"

"Only Dylan could find something to rhyme with Mozambique" he yells at Jens, "and he's never even been here."

Jens, head lolling against the strut, a bottle of Laurentina in his hand. "How do you know that"?

"What?"

"That Dylan's never been here?"

"I just don't see it, man. Why would you come here if the capitals of the world are clamouring for you?

"Here, the women are better," Jens says.

Four storeys high in the abandoned East German-built office block, Jens shouts "CAMARADA" at a knot of men off in a corner. They step back into the shadows, all but one, who steps forward, sweat-stained red t-shirt, cut off sleeves, thick-veined labourer's arms, deep black, a slash of a smile in the dark. Him and Jens clasp hands and bump chests and exchange greetings in Portuguese. With slapped hands, they do the business. A bag of Mozambique Red for a clutch of notes. They linger for a while, sitting on a fallen concrete pillar with reinforced steel coming out of the end like the severed tentacle of a giant octopus, smoking zols[5] rolled in newspaper. Noticias. They drink too, some reeking milky slime that makes him want to retch. Then they're off, clattering back through the rain-slicked steaming streets going nowhere in particular, that universal 2am shoooosh of

---

[5] Fat, homemade marijuana cigarettes.

tires on wet tarmac, nobody else around. Could be Kiev or Lima. Vodka or Pisco Sours.

> *I like to spend some time in Mozambique*
> *The sunny sky is aqua blue*
> *And all the couples dancing cheek to cheek*
> *It's very nice to stay a week or two*
> *And maybe fall in love, just me and you*[6]

Driving back, the occasional moth-bombed lamp, some towers, so hammered at one point the boulevard seems to split into three. He takes the middle one.

The next day. the plane they have been waiting for suddenly becomes available. Reports of a worsening famine have reached the capital, and the government decides it's time to try and get a handle on it, including showing the world the starving thousands to trigger desperately needed aid. They need images to counter the anti-communist blockade. There are so many disasters in Mozambique they have a Minister for the Prevention and Control of Natural Calamities. Amos Mahanjane tells us "these are black lives. We are Marxists. Reagan, Thatcher and Botha want to make us weak. Never!"

At a military airport outside Maputo, a spanking new Antonov makes ready to take a grab-bag of real do-gooders and pretend do-gooders, spooks and hacks, as it will turn out, up north to the famine. A Swedish daily newspaper guy, a Norwegian Trotskyist freelancer, and

---

[6] "Mozambique" Bob Dylan

an elderly American in another white suit and dark shades. He has accreditation from US Aid.

They are all under the control of Mahanjane, a one-time mineworker in SA. He has a face of both profound kindness and enormous hardness. It reminds Rategan of a Detroit Tiger outfielder, Jeffrey Leonard who had the nickname "Penitentiary Face". Amos, who had been picked up and tortured by South African police, had that face. Rategan has seen it in men who have survived the worst conditions life can throw at a person. But Amos escapes South Africa, becomes a guerrilla leader for Frelimo (Frente de Libertação de Moçambique) and is captured. He suffers another spell of imprisonment and torture at the hands of the even nastier Portuguese colonial authorities, before the Portuguese collapse like a cheap suitcase. Now he finds himself one of the drivers of his new nation. His portfolio of natural calamities keeps him busy. Here in the People's Republic of Mozambique floods, drought, disease, civil war, malaria, crop failure, famine and corruption follow hard upon each other in the birthing years of the new nation.

They are stuck at the airport for half a day and Rategan gets to know Amos Mahanjane. Rategan asks him why he thinks there are so many bad things happening to Mozambique.

He points at the sun.

"The South Africans are controlling the sun. They make the sun dry up the clouds. The clouds bring rain. So there is no rain. No rain, no food. Crops die, animals die.

People die. The South Africans are killing the people through the sun."

"What?"

"The South Africans are controlling the sun."

"How can that be, Mr Minister?"

"Their scientists control the sun, and they do not want the People's Mozambique to live. They use chemicals. From planes"

"Can you do anything about that?"

"We can wait."

"Wait for what?"

"Soon it will be over for them, and then we can start."

"Ah."

"We have time. We have had 300 years of whites, before that centuries without them. We can wait a few more years. When the whites are gone, South Africa is free, it begins. A new age for all of Africa."

Turfloop 1971.

So now they've been arrested.

Rategan's body chills in the heat. He's had this feeling before, after getting caned at school, or after a fight. A freezing feeling in the spine, a clarity in the head.

This arrest focuses and accelerates the process of making him who he will become. Though there is fear, it is a great relief. The young Rategan had been artificial. There is Rategan before this moment, and Rategan after. The young Rategan had been artificial. His future is all after this arrest, his past on the other side of it. He is in a corridor, on a wooden bench, waiting his turn with the commanding officer. On the surface it seems like a locking up, descent into unfreedom. In truth it is the opposite, an unlocking, the beginning of his freedom.

Jeannette comes out, sits down next to him on the bench. She puts a current through him, the power of which he feels, though he doesn't understand it. Yet. Her calmness is reassuring.

"Just answer in monosyllables. Yes or no. We are getting lawyers, in Jo'burg."

What he does know in this moment is that he is prepared die for this woman.

"Rategan Edwardes," a voice says.

His turn in the warrant officer's office, Swanepoel, or Engelbrecht or Labuschagne or Goosen, whatever the fuck this one's name is.

Rategan is seething with privileged white boy indignation, trembling with the physical desire to drive his fastest meanest shot right back at Goosen's face and see the terror in his eyes before he ducks and rolls.

"Mr Edwardes?"

"Yes."

"Mr Rategan Edwardes of 130 Maria Street, Sandown Johannesburg?"

"Yes."

"You are being charged under section 12 of the General Assemblies Act, being in a Bantu Trust area without a permit."

"I didn't know I needed a permit to attend church with other South Africans."

More than one syllable, he thinks.

Whatever-his-name-is looks slowly up at Rategan. His expression says, profoundly, he doesn't give a shit what Rategan thinks. His loathing for this privileged English-speaking white boy is palpable. He may be descended from Afrikaners who Rategan's forebears put in history's first concentration camps, during the Boer War. A mere two generations ago. No love lost there, for sure.

He tears off a copy of the charge from the form in front of him.

"You owe the state 20 rand. You will be released on your own recognisances."

"OK."

He scribbles something.

"Next."

That Sunday in Pietersburg, it takes time to process everyone. By the time they leave for Johannesburg, five hours south, they would be taking tea at the cricket.

They are shoved in the back of a VW Kombi. Behind is a brown police Chevvy, and in front a white paddy wagon with the black detainees. Jeannette has the seat in front of him.

It has been a long day.

He falls asleep happily watching her thick curls bouncing along with the bumps in the road.

He wakes to a nudge.

Night time, city streets.

"Where are we?" he asks.

"Pretoria."

She points leftwards towards a large building.

"That's Marshall Street Prison," she says, leaning over the back of her seat, the streetlights catching her lips. And then to all.

"Hey that's Marshall Street, where they're holding Winnie. And it's her birthday."

The whole bus starts singing "Happy Birthday"

When it gets to the Winnie part, the police guy in the front seat swings around with his RAP 401.

"Shut up! Shut Up. This is a banned person."

They hum the rest.

Rategan will never forget the smile on Jeannette's face, her eyes gleaming at the cop's anxiety and helplessness, her face strobing under the passing streetlights.

A steel jacaranda.

He has come through something and is bonded for life. He leans forward.

"Jeannette … Jeannette," he whispers loudly.

She slides across the seat, her face close.

"Who's Winnie Mandi…"

After raising her eyebrow, she tells him the whole story of the Mandelas, a story he doesn't know. He's been taught about Napoleon and Churchill, but not a word about Nelson and Winnie. The mention of their name, their organisation, anything ANC, is banned. As she tells him, her voice fills his ears, his mouth and heart, and conviction replaces the vacuum inside him.

August 1982. In Inhambane, the famine area in Mozambique, they are on a country road, in the back of an open truck, with the government militia, Frelimo. There's been a report of a village attack by Renamo, an armed insurgency secretly funded by apartheid money via the Rhodesian Central Intelligence Organisation.

The government militia takes them to a village. A raggedy bunch with worn clothes, rusty old. 303 hunting rifles and pangas. Two huts burned to cinders, still smoking. Clothes strewn on the ground. A yapping, skeletal cur. Nobody around. They inspect, patrol and confer with a shattered looking woman, a child on her back. She points. They speed away in pursuit, Rategan banging from side to side with the armed men in the back of the truck. He hears two cracks and a ping, the soldiers yell, the truck veers. He copies the men around him as they throw themselves flat in the truck, screaming at the driver to accelerate.

They stay there, lying down on the rattling floor of the speeding truck until they reach the famine camp. Clearly not in control anywhere here.

In the woods hundreds of stick people dawdle. Listless. Or lie in the shade. Mouths open, eyes wide. They have walked for miles through the bush to the coast. A volunteer nurse from the Irish Red Cross supervises a feeding station, a big can of broth steaming over an open fire. Her face is ghostly in the dark leafless wood, her accent lilting with the shuffling of feet and soft moans and whispers around her.

"We have six hundred refugees here today. Every day about fifty walk in from the bush. We don't have enough of anything. Food, medicines, shelter. They are fleeing the fighting and the famine. Everyone tells us stories of people who die along the way. Some have been walking for five days. The situation is worse than critical."

Rategan interviews three refugees, two men and a woman, the thinnest people he has ever seen.
"There is no food."
"Renamo chased us, stole our things, what we had."
"No rain for … before the last time."
"Cattle. Goats." A wiping gesture of a bony arm "Gone. All gone."

He feels an ominous shiver. He has caught something.

Walking from the black wood of the dying back to the village, he sees a pile of rags by the road. It is a baby, still breathing, abandoned. He bends over, peers. It could be a few months old, the skin creased, stressed, like an old person, next to a flickering eye. He takes a photograph, a thin vein beating against the paper skin of its temple. He does this.

And he also does this. He takes out his microphone, presses play and record. He wants to record the sound of the breaths. The last, rattling breaths.

The infant's eyes react to his movement. The helpless white eye twinges, afraid and unable to make the rest of its body move, too weak to protect itself from this shadow that looms.

He will remember this for the rest of his life, like Thandi and the baby who will live, and the steel jacaranda under the lights of Pretoria.

He can see its face now, its eye flickering once towards the approaching mike. This child will die. At his feet. He looks around. There is no one to help. Bodies move listlessly off in both directions, away from this flickering life.

He detests himself. And his parasitic profession. Recording this death, not stopping it. Not knowing how to stop it.

He is no helicopter pilot, he is thinking. He is no doctor. He is a journalist and he will record it. That's all he chooses to do. A truck comes along. He waves it to stop, but it rattles on by, the driver glancing knowingly and disinterestedly, at the shape at his feet.

He walks on now marked by the shame of witness. The witness who did nothing. The witness who does nothing.

He is the World, he thinks, the World that has no excuses. The World at breakfast, on a train, at a bus stop, that sees this picture, again of a nameless, doomed child.

He is a key part of the betrayal of the human race, it's great essential failing. And it is his failing, very much so; a death for which he will always, for the rest of his days, be responsible.

Later that night, with the Swedish newspaper guy, the Norwegian woman, and the American aid man, they talk and drink. Amos tells them the Antonov will not be back to pick them up for three more days. They are stuck here now for three days longer than planned.

The next morning lighters are bringing emergency grain ashore to the wharf alongside the ex-hotel where they are staying. The USAID man in the white suit has introduced himself as Cyrus. Cyrus Clark 111. He stands astride the shipment bobbing in the sea swell, flicking the ash from his Camel; apportioning USAID sacks to freelance truckers who buzz around like desperate flies. They are counting crisp US dollars.

"First step to recovery." Clark drawls, "Freelance capitalism. Small businessmen are the saviours of failed states, the restorers of capital and civilised values to the corpse of Marxist dictatorships. Comrade."

The journalists and Clark are down to eating army rations, Czech canned goods bought from some morose East Germans in a trailer. The East Germans, construction engineers, say they have been abandoned by their own government without provisions or money for nine months. Yet they offer what they have.
They're all sick, diaorrhea and sweats.

Rategan feels the ominous shudder, whatever he picked up from Death Wood. He has inhaled, or ingested something real bad. That night he starts to get sick. He gets worse, quickly. Real, real sick. For thirty-six hours on a wire bed, no mattress, in a room dripping with salt. slime and scuttering with rats, every ounce of liquid thrown up or shat out, every drop of sweat.

In the worst of the delirium the American appears at the side of his bed. He's about sixty, has a red pointy face, greased-back thin black hair, and the somewhat worse-for-wear white jacket. Dark, dark glasses with gold rims, like the spooks in the Spy versus Spy comic strip. Like a guy you want to get out of the office, into the field, far away.
Rategan never sees his eyes.
"How ya' doin?'"
"I feel like a sixteen-clawed hellcat is inside me, shredding my guts," he croaks.
The spy pulls out a battered silver flask, shoves it towards Rategan.
He sips. It sears through him like petrol.
"Bourbon" he drawls.

Again he shoves it at Rategan.

"That'll kill the cat. And it's all the med'cine we got"

On the wall opposite Rategan there's a faded mural of a massive swordfish in full flight, a hook in its mouth, either grinning or grimacing, Rategan can't tell which. The fish is sculpted in relief against painted surf and sea and islands. It had been a resort hotel in the 1950s. "Hemingway was here. Said it was the best marlin fishin' he'd ever seen" -- like he'd been there. And who knows, he may have.

Towards the end of the occupation of his guts by the 16-clawed hellcat, he dreams of Thandi. She is reminding him what Murray Levine says.

"Everyone knows," she is saying impatiently, as if speaking to a fool, "that ninety percent of rural Africans sleep under the stars."

In his fevered state, he rolls off his metal springs in the middle of the night and stumbles outside, under the African stars. He lies down beyond the East German's trailers on the dirt, amidst some bushy thorn trees. Within minutes ants start pricking and stinging his exposed ankles, hands, neck and head. Bats flop through the branches above him like velvet rags, squeaking and diving. He tries to concentrate on the stars. He hallucinates about the pile of rags at the side of the road, now still.

The stars pulse above him.

The fever ebbs.

The trip to the famine camp in Inhambane was supposed to take 48 hours. But they are stuck there for five long, sickening, death-palled days. The disgruntled East German engineers in the trailer cough up enough rice and tea for cash to get them by, while blacks in the nearby leafless, black-boughed forest die of starvation, forty a day.

The day before they leave, the Norwegian Trotskyite bends to Rategan's fevered ear. Whenever she comes by he hears the immortal words of the Stranglers.

> *"That Leon Trotsky*
> *he got a pickaxe*
> *between his shoulders*
> *No More Heroes anymore"*

She is blunt, fingering the silver studs along the edge of her ear. Pretty and macho at the same time. She smells good. "I think I may live," he thinks to himself. "The American" she whispers "is not who he says he is. He's CIA. Based in Washington. Cyrus Clark is not his real name. He's here to do whatever he can to fuck up the Marxists. Did you hear them last night?"

"No. I was out of it."

"Boats. I went and watched them. Clark was there handing out US dollars. They unloaded crates, Wooden crates."

"Weapons, you think?"

"What else."

Although the Trotskyites he had come across over the years were half-crazed, he totally believes her. He figures Clark may have paid Frelimo the government militia, to stay away. A couple of crates delivered to Renamo could create a lot of terror. AKs, so it can be blamed on the Russians.

It's clear Clark is flipping the emergency food through the truck drivers to the Irish nurses in the famine camp, who have no choice but to pay the marked-up price. Clark's grain is saving lives, but that is of secondary importance to his eco/military/political mission. To arm and sustain a pro-American, anti-Soviet network to replace a Frelimo that is, apart from the Minister of Natural Calamities, nowhere to be seen. And it was also those fucking sunglasses he wore. Only a gringo field spook could have such taste.

When the Antonov finally returns, the airport has no professional security. Just the same Frelimo boys from the burned village in their raggedy T-shirts and old. 303s. Rategan re-hears the sound of the weapon that had strafed the truck. Brrrrt, zinnnng. Automatics.

There are about fifty desperate refugees swarming the tiny airport terminal. A rumour has gone around the Antonov will fly them out, south to Maputo, a mercy flight, to food and housing and hospitals.

The American says: "They don't have a prayer. There's not enough room, and there's no-one in Maputo to save them either." He turns to me and hands me a business card. Cyrus C. Clarke 111 US Aid Chevy Chase MD USA. Phone number.

"If you ever get to DC give me a call."

The refugees in the terminal start to murmur, raise themselves from the parquet floor, and point to the sky at the incoming plane. The raggedy unit of soldiers takes up guard between where the Antonov will end up and the people.

When the plane gets in, it turns around, opens its rear door, and unloads supplies for the famine workers. When that is done, the visitors walk up the ramp at the back.

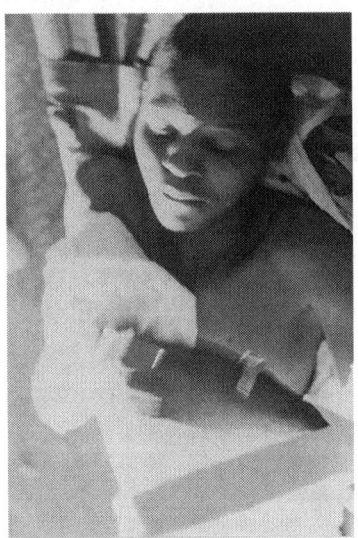

The injured and dying are strapped down among them. Amid the reek of aviation fuel, Rategan can smell the mercurochrome from a mine victim beside him. A brouhaha is flaring on the runway; the rest of the crowd is trying to run around the panicky line of gunmen. The brand-new Antonov has not throttled down and is starting to vibrate and edge forward.

The protective line breaks as the plane moves forward, the rear ramp inching closed. Two or three desperate men, their faces etched in betrayal are reaching for the edge of the closing ramp. Shots ring out.

A man's hand is pinned in the closing door as the plane accelerates. An Irish nurse screams, pointing. The door closes on it. The man next to Rategan, bare body kept together by thick bandages, moans in pain.

Liberation, Rategan thinks, as the plane lifts off and swings out over the palms, and the sand and the resort hotel and Death Wood, out to sea. Liberation. Fingers protrude from the clamped back door. The rest of the man must have fallen off. Onto the tarmac, to survive? Into the sea, for the sharks?

Mahanjane, who has flown in to pick them up, sits across from him, yelling something, and … grinning.

Rategan shakes his head, gesturing to his ears, no hear.

"Did you have a nice visit?" he screams.

Later that year in Washington he takes up Cyrus Clarke's invitation to give him a call, go for a drink. The number is not in service. He calls USAID Africa section. Cy Clarke retired years ago, he is told. They don't know how to contact him now. They haven't had anyone in Mozambique of that name. They believe he passed away a few years back.

Back at the Polana, he is recovering in the air-conditioned room, writing the final script for the radio documentary. There's a knock on the door.
It's Thandi.

He grabs a towel and they head out to the pool, looking over the Indian Ocean.

"So who are you? Really?"
Rategan gives her the Reader's Digest version. The South African back-story, the Canadian "new life," the radio gig, this assignment.

She looks like a model, sipping her Fanta. Then bluntly, directly: "You're not working for the South Africans, are you?"
The allegation. Arrow at the heart. Thunk. So that's what they think.

He wonders if she knows that if he was a spy for Pretoria he would hardly tell her.
"No. I'm not. I was arrested myself in South Africa and expelled. The same year Biko and Curtis and all the others were banned. Paul Pretorius was in my bath when the Security Police came for him. You people,

people like you, in the frontline states, are doing what I would do if ..."

"What" She has narrowed her eyes at the horizon.

"If I didn't mind killing people."

There's a long pause. She puts the drink down, looks over, taking in the Portuguese couple on a chaise longue across the pool, the waiter in his white coat and red fez. She looks back at him. The sun is throwing dancing lights on her face, reflecting off the pool.

"Could I have one of those?" nodding at his Marlboros. Rategan is thinking he'd love to take her inside and wash the sand off her throat.

He flicks a lighter.

"Didn't pick you for a smoker."

"I'm not ..."

It's clear from how she draws on the cigarette that this is one thing that's true. She continues: "Things are strange around here. The place is crawling with informers. There's a list of frontline people that's been handed to some new secret death squad out of Pretoria. No-one is going to help you right now. Since Ruth's death, everyone is very, very ... suspicious."

"Understandable."

She appraises him, softening for the first and only time. "And then you show up."

It hangs in the air. He is reminded how glad he is now to be able to crawl back, tortoise-like, into being a Canadian. He remembers from his past the terrible, corrosive paranoia, the revelations shortly after he was expelled from South Africa about how badly infiltrated all the students' organisations were. The man in charge of funneling all the overseas aid money into South Africa turns out to have been a South African undercover policeman.

As she walks away, he thinks his goose is probably cooked with this lot. And he suspects their secretive ways mask a complete lack of confidence, and discipline. So no matter how honourable one is, somewhere down the line one bad word -- and you're fucked.

The Naval Club, Simonstown
A black waiter in an impeccable white shirt (lots of those still in the new South Africa), burgundy waistcoat, and pin-on black tie serves drinks, sliding a paper coaster with an anchor and cannon logo under their glasses.
Ja Meneer this, Ja Meneer that. Peanuts, chips and olives. Botes the assassin is drinking a Castle. Rategan Canada Dry.

"In some ways," Botes says "it's still the old days," Folding Rategan into that old white man drinking fellowship. At the end of the day, or after the "Revolution" Blacks serve, we drink. Hey? The natural order of things, man.

Now he is a small businessman with two small daughters and a nice little wife.

He raises his glass. "Forgive and forget." Rategan doesn't. "That's what I say, nogal."

Rategan waits until the waiter replaces Botes's beer and he settles back, a wobbly little saint tattoo on his forearm.

"Did you kill Jeannette Curtis?" Rategan says flatly.

"No, not her."

Botes tells his story, with the banality of a post office worker.

"Sachs Ja..him.. I made soup out of his arm.

I don't feel so good about it now, but then. As far as we was concerned, this was a war, these were the enemy, they were on our list, and our job was to eliminate the people who is trying to eliminate us. Same with any other war, anywhere else. Nothing new. Mistakes were made, but their bombs offed a few innocents on our side, too."

He leans forward to stub out his butt in the cut-glass ashtray, looks up. "I guess you're going to ignore those victims, huh?"

"Ahspose u gonna ignor thus viktims"

Botes confesses to being in on "eliminations".

"I dunno, about six. Sometimes you never heard what happened, at the other end."

The deeply brown face from the sun and maybe a touch of the tar brush in the curly dark hair. Peperkorrels (pepper corns). One of the huge ironies of apartheid was that 30 percent of white Afrikaners had coloured blood. So they said. Taut, washboard stomach gone slightly thick in the prosperity of post-apartheid forgiveness.

"Why are you admitting this?"

"My priest says it's good for me." Ma Prisst.

"Get it all out you know. They offered us psychologists, seven hundred rand an hour. On them. Hah. What a load of shit. One of our okes ended up marrying his shrink. Got his money's worth, eh?"

His thick hand brushes imaginary specks off the glass tabletop, rage flashing.

"Nee-man. They screwed us. The fokking politicians, the generals. They said they'd back us up, if it … fokked up … well it worked perfectly. We hit our targets. We were good, man …and then, sanctions, the Americans cut us off and they run like rats. They loved us while we were hot. Then they sell out, and we are shit. They still owe us money."

He makes a move as if to spit, but there's a carpet on the nice wooden floor. A blue carpet on the veneered floor with the anchor and cannon design, just lekker and nice. The only emotion he shows. He is momentarily a feral man, snarling in the shadows, just inviting someone to poke him too hard.

It wasn't going to be Rategan. He ran his tongue over his false tooth, or often fingered the break in his nose, or the bump on his left rib where Afrikaners like Botes had made contact in the past. Head-butts, punches. He hadn't clashed with anyone tougher. Well maybe some Russian Mafia guys in Sebastopol, but that's another story. He'd seen bull terriers and Afrikaners fight, swarming their victims, the rising, mounting back, the pecking, blurred fusillade of fist and tooth and claw.

"Botes's backstory is typical. Born on a struggling white farm in the back of beyond, in the Karroo, through a hardscrabble hoërskool, to the army. His bush skills and sniping are noticed and he's picked for Special Forces. Sniper and explosives expert. Serves behind lines in Angola, propping up Unita, trying to keep communism and the Cubans at bay, "where things got nasty".

Then back to Pretoria to a secret organisation euphemistically called the Civil Co-operation Bureau, the government office on the fourth floor of a nondescript building in Pretoria from whence flow the parcel and car bombs.

It's the banality of evil, institutionalised.

The soft landing of the Guerrilla Killer.

Yachts through the window behind him, loll in the swell, the clack of halyard and stay in the constant Cape winds.

One of Rategan's journeys is over. With a ginger ale, not a bang. What had he expected?

There is either revenge or forgiveness. He could comfortably hide his hatred or murderous intent before the face of this deeply tanned bang-bang boy with the berry-brown eyes. Rategan could see the man's Ouma[7] pinching those cheeks, back in the day.

"Isn't he a little sweetie"?

Rategan stands up. A bit abrupt, but time to leave.

Standing above him, Rategan senses Botes, like an attack dog, sniffing the wind.

"You done?"

---

[7] Granny

"Done."

He seems a little disappointed. He's enjoying the attention, Rategan thinks.

He stands up and offers his hand. Rategan takes it, anticipating the fierce grip.

"You know, like I say, you will not identify me in your Canadian documentary, and especially my store, and where I live. I have a new life. It's a new South Africa."

He smiles. It's not a friendly smile. He lets go of Rategan's hand, then raises one finger at Rategan's face.

"But allow me to absolutely clear about this one thing. We are still very close, me and my unit, around South Africa.

'Infandum Mors.' 'Beyond Death.'

"If we are poked by anybody, ever, we can cause massive damage. OK?"

Rategan looks him in the eye.

"Massive damage. To this whole country. In a heartbeat, my friend."

Rategan pulls out some money for the drink. Botes places a hand on his.

"Please, my friend. It's on me."

She opens the parcel in Lobango.
She opens the door in Maputo.

She opens the parcel in Lobango, and birds fly off the roof of the apartment building. Angolans know what that is. There's the sound of running footsteps. A scream, maybe several. Jeannette Curtis and her daughter are over.

Across the continent, in Maputo, Thandi opens the door, and with one hand on it, the other around her baby, looking at me. A few blocks away an office lay echoing from a bomb.

Rategan's assignment in Mozambique is the famine, not the ANC in exile. But any excuse in a storm, to get back there, back turned to the mostly indifferent Canadian audience, hurtling towards where the heart of the fire for justice and truth beats in the African bush and its noisy, busted frontline cities.

If he'd been true to his political emotions, Rategan should have joined the ANC long before he left and joined the CBC, fought for his real country.
He just didn't think they were going to win, and Canada was the safe choice. They have The Queen, and English, and a democracy.

If the ANC and Mandela in the end hadn't won, bad would have triumphed over good. He left again, and eventually, so did Thandi. Fled to Canada
They met years later at a dinner party in a very upmarket part of Toronto. A lot of his heart was not there. She had brought what was left of her heart, her beauty intact and had moved on finding refuge in Canadian academe. She said people in Toronto wouldn't know, or care where a place called Mozambique was.

Of the people in this story the victimized never completely recovered. The only one left behind, and prospering, is the killer.

DOCUMENTARIES:

Radio. Mozambique 1987 CBC Sunday Morning. (CASS 18/25)

Television: "By Persons Unknown" w Martin Seemungal: The Journal CBC TV VHS 3

CBC TV Madiba: The Life and Times of Nelson Mandela DVD 1.

2 RATEGAN DOES SALVADOR

He'd taken a course in the history of art at university in South Africa so he knows what a truly beautiful woman looks like. But he'd never seen a real live one until that night at the booze can on Queen Street West in Toronto.

She is leaning against a wall, captured in a pool of light from above, a glass in her hand. Thick wavy black hair, big eyes, laughter tumbling out. She remains a vision that disappears into the crowd until, when he is leaning against the same wall listening to the cool boys, she re-emerges out of the dark, steps in front of him and plants a big kiss right on his mouth. Leaves it there for a while, steps back a foot and just looks, her big moist eyes deep into him. You have been chosen, they are saying.

About bloody time, he thinks.

Now, a rich year later, as he rocks in the back seat of the limo, purring towards the Airport, the cocaine blue metal taste on the back of his tongue, he is escaping the spectacular train-smash of the affair. Rategan knows he is in exactly the sort of shape required for a shitty, lethal little war that raises some good old moral dilemmas. The sort of barely relevant blip on world history that could take you down with it. The sort of restorative exercise needed to anaesthetize his Northern agony.

About thirty-six hours before, at four in the morning, Sandy, the executive producer shows him the chair in his cramped office in the radio building, previously a convent in downtown Toronto.

He's just come from hearing Rategan's first piece, about a born-again Hell's Angel. At the first pass, in that same office, earlier that night, on an old playback machine, he had okayed the piece for broadcast.

"Did you hear the cat?" Rategan asked.

"What cat?"

"You didn't hear the cat?"

"No."

"When the godly biker is talking on the phone to the kid in intensive care in Peterborough."

The EP looks at him with an expression of contained impatience. He's got to vet a three-way debate on Federal politics, take in the feed from Fisk in Beirut, and record all the bells and whistles.

"No, I missed it. But it's good enough. Go now."

Later in the studio, mixed and sweetened, you can hear the cat's meows, between the gravelly voice of the evangelical Biker talking to a dying kid. Rategan re-sees the scar-faced brindle Tom walking across the black leather shoulders, meowing perfectly in the pauses between the man's tender words.

"The Lord is with you (meow) He walks with you and me (meow) taking you to eternal peace (meow) the most beautiful place ever."

Now, as the show goes out live to Newfoundland in the freezing Canadian dawn, the Executive Producer says to Rategan,

"C'mon here."

They find a place in the corridor.

"Did you hear the cat??"

"Yeah, yeah, I heard the cat."

The EP, a guy with wire brush curls and exhausted green eyes, sets his face close to Rategan's.

"Listen."

He hands him a New York Times clipping about US military aid to Central America.

"Go to El Salvador. Get behind enemy lines. Get this story."

Rategan stares at it, mute.

"If you do, I'll get you the Order of Canada."

His foreign editor in Toronto, in a former life, had been the Canadian coordinator of support for the various left-wing networks in Central and South America. After sliding shut the glass door in one of those tiny editing suites in the old convent building, and saying it would be better if Rategan keeps the following to himself, he gives Rategan an intense 15-minute briefing about the Salvadorean opposition, civilian and military. Rategan reduces it to a hand-sized page of letters and names. FMLN- ERP (Farabundo Marti Liberation Front-Ejercito Revolucion Partido) is headed by a guy called JV (Joaquin Villalobos). So he writes, in his beloved Parker fountain pen FMLN-ERP on one side of the spiral-top-sized page, and JV on the other. He does the same with the five others. The FDR, the FPL, RN, PRTC, PCS, revolutionary or semi-revolutionary groups all financed by Marxist/Communist or Socialist states.

"You'll get into Mexico City tomorrow night. Go straight to the Casa Azul. Eight ayem Friday morning there will be a red-headed woman in the courtyard. Her name is Louise. Do what she says. If she isn't there by ten a.m., get onto the first flight to Salvador. Learn the list. Then destroy it. Okay? That's important."

On the way to Mexico City, Rategan memorizes all the names and acronyms.

He checks into the Casa Azul, which, from the front, looks like a fairly nondescript pensione with a small blue ceramic nameplate in a front passageway. A few paces through the cool is a sun-blasted courtyard, skies of blue painted on the walls, beautifully carved wooden tables and chairs separated by thick tropical bushes with drowsy pink and white blooms, with the odd fluttering butterfly.

The next morning, on the dot, the woman is there. A Quebecoise. She asks if he slept well, then crooks her finger. He follows her out. They drop down into a nearby subway. Three stops later they emerge and walk a few blocks and into the back of an empty small white sedan with blackened windows. On the seat next to him there is a pair of black eye blinkers. She tells him to put them on. Somebody gets in the driver's side, and he hears a man's voice as they drive off. After a journey of fifteen minutes there's a bumpy section, the car draws to a stop, and a garage door slides shut behind him.

"You can remove the eye blinds," she whispers.

She walks him into a suburban bungalow to a sunny room where three men sit around a table. They are the civilian leaders of the biggest guerrilla force in the Salvadorean civil war. Ruben Zamorra and Ernesto Schmidt he recognizes. The third he doesn't. They talk for a while in Spanish, the niceties, the courtesies, the introductions, a bit about comparisons to the South African struggle that piques their interest. Popular uprisings and insurrecciones.

The touristy prints on the wall of matadors and folk dancers suggest this is more of a safe house than a base.

The briefing formally starts. For the next 45 minutes Zamorra speaks in almost perfect English, giving what seems to Rategan an eminently sensible, if social democratic, analysis of the state of the war, the origins of the FMLN, the socio-economic history of El Salvador, the quatorze familias, the role of American coffee and fruit companies, the current role of the US military, the death squads, the whole shebang.

This will not be the last time Rategan is profoundly impressed by how deeply people think about their own countries and how beautifully they express it. Over the years he will hear it from educated, sensitive men and women, often lawyers or teachers or union leaders, exiled or inside, and in mortal danger from South Africa, Iran, China, Peru, Cuba, the USA and on.

They live in a special world. Often ripped from victimized families, they have taken that fork in the road. Armed struggle over working to overturn the system from within. There's blood and eruption in their backstories. They are full of contradictions, about class, race, education and commitment.

Over the years several of these brilliant and patriotic people that he has met die gruesomely: parcel bombs, drive-by shootings, poisonings, carried out by doomed leaders prepared to murder to stay in power.

He has half a dozen questions which they answer patiently, defining areas he cannot go, including where they get their money and weapons. For him, these briefings are worth a thousand scoop interviews with Presidents who are so heavily processed they rarely say anything human at all. The intimately informed insider provides him with the raw material. It underpins the shape he will give to the documentary, the sequences, the images, the sounds, and the arguments he will present. Take a couple of scenes from the other side, and it's balanced and informative, packaged for free for millions of listeners in Canada and the US and beyond.

They will not connect him with a guerrilla leader inside the country, but, as the third, unnamed man says, the corners of his mouth turning up into a smile,

"We know where to find you."

Fair enough, Rategan thinks. Their war, for me just a story.

As he stands up and shakes hands, they apologize for the eye blind. Rategan says he understands, and would have no idea how to re-find them, or explain it to anyone else. There's a little freezing there, and Rategan curses himself for inferring a re-telling of this meeting. This is not social: this is life and death, he thinks, as they bump along in the dark and the car eventually hits smooth asphalt, and the thrum of the city engulfs them.

Back then, the powers in Canadian broadcasting seemed to think telling a Canadian audience about these places, in this way, was worth the expense. Now Rategan sees that has changed. Canada has gone from aiding liberators to backing companies that arm the anti-liberators. And long-form documentaries on the national networks are dead and gone. Maybe the main source of thoughtful scrutiny has lost a big source of its information.

Just before leaving for the connecting flight to San Salvador, he flushes the list of guerrillas, armies and their leaders down the toilet at the pensione. He still has no idea how he is going to contact secretly, any one of these guerrilla leaders inside the country.

"Get behind the lines. I'll get you the Order of Canada..." He chuckles.

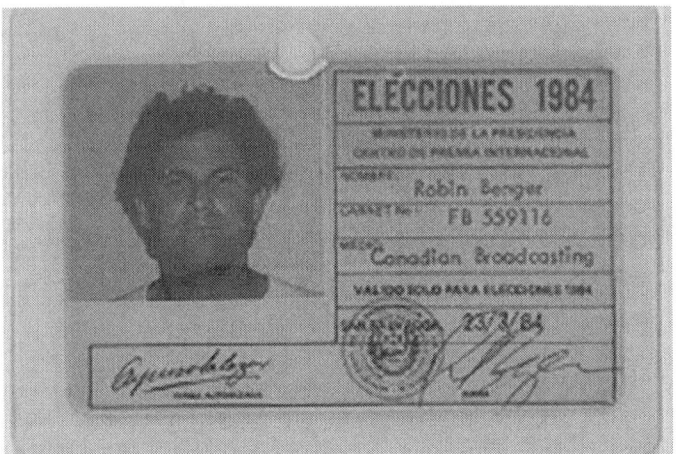

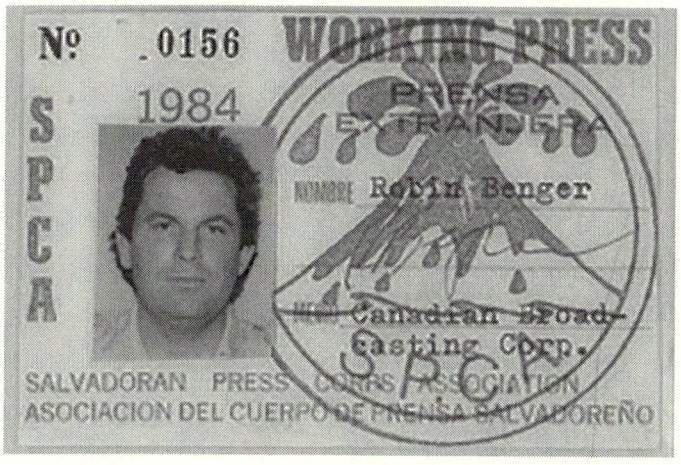

Rategan stands in line at airport customs. Spanish voices and the woman in front of him wearing correspondent's khaki. She hands over a Dutch passport and he hears her say, "Schoemann, Rowena." Then, "New York Times."

"Buenos Dias."

He hands over his Canadian passport.

"Pasaran!"

He goes on through. The sun blasts his winter-worn, love-shattered face. An ember of summer inside him flickers to life. He shuts his eyes, letting the heat sink in. Healing.

The New York Times woman is next to him.

"You heading for the Camino Real?"

"Uh-uhh."

A local is loading her gear into a Mercedes van with black windows.

"Wanna ride?"

"Sure."

It's his first war zone.

El Salvador 1980.

From his 23rd floor hotel room he can see the Volcano. Guazapa. He's wearing khakis, an open shirt. The window is open. He can hear the sounds of the city, motorbikes, the market, kids, wafting up from below. Birdsong and bike horns. Room service coffee on the desk, his notebook, cigarettes, his tape recorder. There's the occasional blurt of machine gun fire from the outskirts.

He's a sole operator. He likes that but he needs someone who knows the lay of the land.

He's rented a scratched-up green Toyota, with PRENSA INTERNATIONALE written in thick red capitals on a big piece of white cardboard on the front window. This, he is told, should make it less likely that either side in the conflict will blow him to bits.

He hires a driver, a sweet guy with bad acne, Fermin.

Hanging around the hotel lobby, he finds a freelancer from Minnesota.

Sam Doyle speaks fluent Spanish.

That first day they get to the other side of the Volcano, but can't pass a military roadblock, and are sent back. Someone has been killed up ahead. They won't give details. Three hours and one life ended. Sam does a few interviews with peasants at the side of the road.

They peel back to the capital and go to the cathedral square where a bunch of protestors had been shot a few days before. A memorial rally for the assassinated Archbishop Romero had erupted. There's still some debris, a plastic sandal, a dirty bandanna on the stones, and Sam points out the smears of blood where protestors dragged their dead and dying comrades into ambulances. Over-weaponed teenage soldiers with downy moustaches stand around, surly, waving the muzzles of their guns to move them on.

With the cicadas singing in the sun-and bullet-blasted courtyard, Rategan senses an atmosphere of nervy anticipation. Even when nothing is actually happening, there's a feeling it's about to happen. Something in the air feels like it could go off at any second. Something that waits, an embryo of running feet and the fusillades of repression. It's just a shout away.

When he gets back to the hotel he goes for a swim. A shapely blonde woman in a bikini, wearing dark glasses, lies in a sun chair. He doesn't disturb her, and dives in. As he makes a turn, he notices a big, blond man with still cameras rushing up to the woman, gesticulating, pointing at the volcano, clearly very upset. After another lap Rategan walks up the steps out of the pool.

"Who the fuck is this." the man says. American.

"I have no idea." she says. Upper class English.

"I'm Rategan Edwardes, from Toronto,

Canadian Broadcasting Corporation."

"Mattison," he says. Rategan has heard of him. Time magazine hotshot.

"How long have you been here?"

"Day and a half."

"Ever covered a war?"

"Nope. Any advice?."

"Fuck off back to Canada"

He storms off.

"Susie Morgan[8]," the woman says.

"The Economist."

They shake hands.

"You don't sound very Canadian," She says, perceptively.

"I grew up in South Africa."

"Thought so. That may have set him off."

"How so?"

"A photographer was just killed in a firefight. With Tim. Ian Mates. They travelled together. He's South African. Was South African."

A bird swoops over the pool, over the wall.

"Yeah. We were up there. Turned back by the military."

Rategan brings the towel up to his face, pushes his eyes into it, hard, for several seconds. Brings it down.

"I'm so sorry…"

---

[8] On May 30 1984 Susie Morgan was seriously injured when a CIA-planted bomb blew up at a news conference for the Contra Leader Eden Pastora in Nicaragua, killing four and maiming her and others. After multiple surgeries she wrote and produced a book and a documentary "In Search of the Assassin"

"Occupational hazard."

That evening, Rowena spots Rategan in the lobby and invites him to dinner with some of her heavyweight American colleagues. There's the foreign editor, the Latin American bureau chief and Rowena. All from the New York Times, the Latin American correspondent from the Boston Globe, and the ubiquitous Martin Bell from the BBC.

The fact they are here in such strength puzzles Rategan a bit, but he keeps his mouth shut most of the time, surrounded by people who have at least ten years on him, the first–timer. Once they hear he's with the Canadian Broadcasting Corporation they seem to decide they have nothing to glean from him, and they are probably right.

After listening to them for a while he is encouraged to learn they think like him. They're also single-mindedly obsessed with the story. Actual description of real events, skirmishes, battles, interrogations, meetings and rumours of meetings and assassination plots. Lots of analytical thinking, which he loves.

They talk on about sources, at State and DOD, the Embassy, the Salvadorean military, and the leftist insurgency. Their knowledge of local politicians and generals is impressive, way beyond his. But they all seem to be focused on feeding their readership's appetite for how all of this affects American interests. As US President Reagan has defined the opposition here as Communist, it's clear that assessing the situation from an objective, democratic perspective is simply not happening. It's flag-waving journalism.

As an English-born South African-Canadian, he relishes the distance this gives him.

Looking at the intense, conversing faces of the American and Brit correspondents now well into their fourth round of drinks, Rategan's conclusion is that he should probably operate away from the Americans. They represent a bad disease, the superpower disease. Nonetheless, here he is, chomping carne quesada with what those three leaders in Mexico may describe as the elitist mouthpieces of US imperialism. To him they sound like a well-informed, reasonable bunch still, dining on the USS Information. After an hour and several drinks the foreign editor of the Times turns to him and says,

"What's your story, Rategan?"

Rategan is struck with an uncharacteristic fit of speechlessness,

"I'm to get behind enemy lines, and make a radio documentary out of it."

The bureau chief, and decorated ex-Vietnam Marine, narrows his eyes and appraises Rategan, Martin Sheen-like.

"You ever covered a war?"

"Nope. Any advice?"

"Three things. Learn the language. Never cross lines. Never travel alone."

Rategan raises his glass,

"Cheers to that. Thanks."

He doesn't reciprocate.

"You don't sound like a Canadian to me."

"Lots of us don't." Rategan answers.

"He's South African," says Rowena

"Now that's a story worth covering," says the foreign editor..

A few nights later, a knock on his door.

It's Rowena. She's wearing night-time camo-fatigues, and smells good.

She needs someone to drive her to a nighttime meeting with "a source". Someone she can "trust", who isn't going to scoop her.

"Ok?"

She shoves the PRENSA INTERNATIONALE sign in the back, and they head out.

As they wind their way under the lush trees of a fashionable neighbourhood, she asks,

"You know what deep background is?"

"I think so."

"You can't name your source... Name or quote. Or his department. Or Location."

"Okay."

"What we are about to do is so deep background, it never happened."

"Well it hasn't even happened yet."

"And it's never going to happen."

A bit Beckettian, thinks Rategan.

"Okay."

"You got to promise me this."

"What."

"If anyone ever asks you about this. It never happened."

"Ok."

"If you have any reservations, tell me now, and you can stay in the car. It's a safe garage, probably the most secure garage in Central America."

(How safe is that, he thinks to himself)

"No reservations," he says.

They eventually turn into a heavily treed drive, out of sight of the road. Palm trees and security lighting. An armed guard with a white helmet watches over them as she talks into a mesh rectangle beneath blackened glass. A crackly voice.

"Proceed."

"Marines," she murmurs, "diplomatic residence."

They are in. They are shown into what strikes Rategan as a luxury apartment, another world from the barrios and hotels of the city.

"This guy is attached to the US Embassy," Rowena says. She seems excited, honing in on something. Rategan senses she loves this part.

A short man with a deep tan wearing a collarless white shirt emerges from a darkened hallway. He holds onto the handshake just a tiny bit too long for Rategan's comfort, like a gay guy fishing for a sign.

"From Canada, huh," the voice soft, nodding slowly. "I actually grew up in upstate New York. Went to the Ex one year."

He introduces himself to Rategan as Ed Garfinkel. He now reminds Rategan of Peter Lorre, the hairline, the bulging eyes, the soft hand. He offers them drinks. They have scotches, Rategan, dark rum. Garfinkel, definitely not his real name, walks over to the big plate glass window at the opposite side of the room, makes sure the curtain is completely closed, and fiddles with a cassette machine.

The opening bars of Don McLean's "American Pie" starts up.

Garfinkel.

Rategan wonders whether he should have used a false name too.

Mandrake. Garth.

"Garfinkel" settles into a white leather couch in front of them, American Pie playing behind him, a low black glass table between them.

"So bye-bye, Miss American Pie
Drove my Chevy to the levee, but the levee was dry."

With minimal prompting from Rowena, who fits into all of this like a Siamese cat, he then proceeds to tell them how a man called Roberto D'Aubuisson has carried out the assassination of Archbishop Romero.

Romero is celebrating mass at a hospital chapel for the terminally ill. A red car draws up. A man appears at the door of the chapel and fires one, maybe two shots.

The assassin is paid 1000 Salvadorean colons[9] by Roberto D'Aubuisson.

Garfinkel's delivery is unerring, soft, but military, Rategan is thinking. American Pie is on a loop. Don McLean starts up again.

Is it to frustrate any bugs?

"Want another one?" Garfinkel asks Rowena. She pushes her cut glass tumbler towards him. As Garfinkel goes over to the drinks cabinet, Rowena pulls out a small spiral notebook and makes a couple of notes with a short yellow pencil with an little pink eraser that she's pulled out of her shirt pocket.

Garfinkel is back with the two tumblers full of scotch, and continues, unfazed by the notebook. He purrs on, his words as clear as pebbles dropped into a pool.

The shooter is a man called Regalado, D'Aubuisson's head of security.

"Them good old boys were drinkin' whiskey and rye

---

[9] @200 US$

Singin' "This will be the day that I die
This'll be the day that I die"

On the Sunday just past the sniper is playing soccer in Guazapo and D'Aubission pulls him off the field, puts him in the back of his Landcruiser, takes him to the airport, tells him he's going to Miami. To a safe house, where his wife and kids will join him.

But the plane banks southwest instead of northeast and five miles out of San Salvador they shoot him in the back of the head and throw his body into the Pacific.

Falling man, spiraling down, his children now fatherless.

Rategan wants to ask how they keep the bodies down. This is all dreamlike now. He is seeing the cassock crumpling, a body falling, falling through the sky, the splash, the silence, the receding plane noise, the expressions of the men in the plane, set for home.

He vaguely hears Rowena ask the American some questions, along the lines of who knew what. Garfinkel says the Americans didn't know anything about it until D'Aubuisson's pilot, in a ploy to get US citizenship and a house in Florida, spills the beans.

"And while Lenin read a book on Marx
A quartet practiced in the park
And we sang dirges in the dark
The day the music died"

The Don McLean song keeps on repeating. Rategan knew he would hate the song from this day on. It is the first of several times he realizes fascists and killers love his music too. Springsteen has been responsible for a lot of mayhem with that "Born in the USA". He is also feeling alive, alive, alive. On one level he is getting the scoop on the most important story of the day. Inside he is astonished at the soft arrogance of it all, the murderous economy of thought and action, the rapidity of it, but not surprised at his luck. He's always had luck.

When they are done, they shake hands. In a day or two Ed is leaving for his next posting "somewhere" in the Middle East. He raises his finger. "Just wait a second," he says, disappearing into the apartment. He comes back with an old two flag friendship button.

"Give my best to the EX. I saw Guess Who there. You know Nancy Reagan banned their song American Woman from the White House?"

"No I didn't."

"Have this." he says. The Maple Leaf and the Stars and Stripes, crossed, with CNE 1968 scrolled across the flagsticks.

"No I couldn't." says Rategan. He pins it on Rategan's war zone waistcoat.

"Until we meet again, comrade." he winks, and guides them outside.

On the way back, Rategan concentrates on getting safe through the streets of San Salvador to the hotel.

Fear fills the shadows. It is the kind of place, the first of several places he would drive or walk through, where you are driving along and you hear the sound of a volley of bullets being fired somewhere around the city. He finds it strangely comforting. He feels like, in the rootlessness of the place, even the bursts of distant violence, he is home. He feels he will never feel that way in stable, routine places. Hot places, with revolution in the air: for him this is home.

In the parking lot of the hotel, with its palm-treed islands and moths bombarding the lamps, they sit in the darkness in the car.

"That was an incredible story. Who was that guy?"

"The CIA station chief."

"Ahaa."

"That's what deep background is, eh? He gets his story out and it's not traceable."

"That's it. What did you think?"

"Amazing. My small question. How far is it from the chapel door to where the Archbishop was standing, at the altar. My big question. Was D'Aubuisson acting on his own?"

"Well Reagan's people and his people, the ARENA people, have the same objective..."

"They don't want this place going Commie, right? And didn't the NYT report that Arena's backers are getting money from right-wingers in the US"

"Lots of it. That's why (the foreign editor) is here"

A man in a shimmering white shirt crosses under a lamplight in front of them, and into the hotel.

"And they want D'Aubuisson to become President?"

A cat darts into the shadows of the garden. Rategan is perturbed. He has come a long way in a very short time.

Three days and he has just spent an evening in the brains of this war.

"What are your plans tomorrow?", Rowena asks

He looks at her. She's attractive, in a mannish way. He loves a woman of the world, tough, can handle herself, comfortable in a war zone. Short brown hair. A nose that had been flattened sometime. Brown eyes. Dark skin. Maybe she was from one of the Dutch colonies.

Half-Moluccan maybe, the daughter of an Indonesian magnate and his Dutch mistress.

"Ahh. Sam has a lead on something," he murmurs. "I'm going off with him."

"What's that?"

"You know, I appreciate you taking me along tonight. Letting me ride on your amazing contacts. But Sam has asked me to say nothing. And to tell you the truth I know very little about it. He just said six ayem."

"I understand. If you told me I'd be worried about you talking about tonight."

"Naa. It's cool," he replies.

She opens the door and they get out. "You gonna have a drink?"

"No," taking in the decibel level of the bar with a wince he says. "Not my style."

"Think I will."

"Okay."

She turns away.

"And Rowena. Thanks a lot for tonight"

She inclines her head the tiniest bit, and is gone.

He avoids the bar, which is full of big-name, loud-voiced male journos drunkenly debriefing and decompressing. He'd been there the night before. He'd gotten drunk with a guy called Hoagland, a hotshot freelance photographer who already had one Newsweek and one Time cover to his name. He was a scrawny long-haired Californian, Rategan's first real live fuck-you hard-rockin' Calfornian. It was the kind of place and the kind of drinking where honesty comes on to you like a runaway horse.

"How much experience should you have?" Rategan had asked him, trusting his advice immediately, instinctively, "to cover wars like this?"

"I'm a b-and-e artist from Southern California. I had busted into my stepfather's electrical supply warehouse and on the way out, lit it up real good and got caught; I was doing community service, and I stole 200 bucks from the old bastard, bought a camera, and hitched down here 18 months ago."

"But don't you need all sorts of military and political and linguistic knowledge?"

He laughed and leaned in.

"Here it is and you can have it for free. The local military are a bunch of trigger-happy cunts run by the US; the guerrillas are mostly from poor backgrounds, most of them just want the death squads to stop and the US to go home; there wouldn't be a war here at all if Reagan's crowd hadn't framed it up as the next Red Tide about to swamp suburban Minneapolis. But... the weather, the food and the women are great, Spanish is pretty easy for me-I'm living with a local, so..."

Suddenly, an obnoxious veteran of 'Nam and Suez and Congo and Nigeria, like Rategan a guy who'd clearly been raised white in South Africa, grabs Rategan and, bottle of bourbon in hand, drags him up to one of the Suites Conquistadores, where he watches middle-aged war correspondents drink and gamble. At dawn they would all leave in varying states of disrepair to cover "the bang bang" in military choppers. It held no appeal to him. The story, yes, the story grabbed him. But their cynicism was corrosive, and the plugging into the worst possible expectations of their reader-viewership, especially around death, nauseated him.

At breakfast two days later a very businesslike Rowena approaches him.

"If you survive this, you'll be a better person for it."

"What do you mean?'

She sits down opposite him, grabs a roll and a packet of marmalade.

"I've heard D'Aubuisson is speaking in Santa Clara, the coffee capital." She says.

Rategan needs an interview with D'Aubuisson, the leader of the right wing party and presidential candidate. Everyone does. His American-press secretary is dicking them around. There's a rumour he is doing a 60 minutes profile and nothing else. It's Wednesday and Rategan has to feed his first doc by Saturday night. It's about human rights abuses and a clip or two from D'Aubuisson, then believed to be running the White Hand Death Squad, would make the trip a success in its first week.

"You bet," he says.

On the drive out there with Fermin, Rowena is at her professional best. She knows all the oligarchs by name, has met half of them, is encyclopedic, even explaining why Salvadorean coffee beans are so profitable and coveted.

She's interviewed D'Aubuisson before and has scrutinized his bank accounts in Miami.

The zocalo in Santa Maria is a riot of bunting, brass bands, strumming guitars, and women in beautiful folkloric dresses; preening, dark-glassed men either on horseback or leaning on Land Cruisers with blackened windows.

D'Aubuisson is a martinet of the Robert Goulet variety, slender, wiry, with a hoarse deep voice. He can work a crowd, especially one this adoring, as well as anyone Rategan has seen. Observing him, Rategan is reminded of a combination of lounge lizard and Goebbels.

Arena flags, blue-red and white with a fat cross ripple in the glorious sunlight. D'Aubuisson talks for too long, revelling in the warm surges of worship from, especially, the women in the crowd. Rategan wonders whether he's a little juiced. He has a reputation, like Sonny in "The Godfather". D'Aubuisson spots Rowena and makes a pointing gesture to her as he disappears amidst a phalanx of security into a hacienda-like house on the square.

After a moment, his American PR guy pops out and says to Rowena, "Five minutes".

The 60 minutes crew, which now seems to be the only other foreign press there, glowers furiously as Rowena and Rategan duck in front of them and into the house.

In a large front living room, there's a scene of bellicose conviviality. D'Aubuisson waves Rowena to a large low leather sofa opposite him across a black glass table. Rategan tags along and he is in. He flips his recorder out and places it on the table, dabbing the 'record' lever.

Over the phone he's told his foreign editor an interview with D'Aubuisson is unlikely, but if he gets a chance to ask him one question, what is it?

"Why did you kill Archbishop Romero?" Michael Findlay had said. Rategan had drawn his breath in, but, after a pause replied.

"Si vous voulez"

Now he is opposite D'Aubuisson who is answering questions in Spanish from Rowena.

When she says, "My friend from Canada would like to ask you a couple of questions," Rategan slides his microphone under D'Aubuisson's chin. D'Aubuisson looks at Rategan, takes a slug from a cut glass with brown liquor, lights a cigarette, sucks in deeply, and says,

"Como No."

He knows this is the moment he cherishes in all of his assignments. Get the Bad guy. In his own small way arrest Evil, advance Good.

"Senor D'Aubuisson. Muchas Gracias. As a future leader of El Salvador, the question most Canadians would have about you is this."

Rategan looks directly into D'Aubuisson's eyes. They are a dead, grey colour.

"Why did you kill Archbishop Romero?"

The room falls completely silent. One of his bodyguards slaps his hand on the stock of his automatic weapon. D'Aubuisson narrows his eyes, now fully fixed on Rategan. He glances down at the recorder, the cassette lazily turning. Slowly his lips part in a snakey grin and suddenly he throws his head back and guffaws.

There is a chorus of laughs from the big men standing around him.

Just as suddenly, the smile disappears, the laughter ends. He sticks his hand around the back of his jeans, and produces a handgun, placing it on the glass table between them with a dull click. The leather couch creaks as Rowena, beside him on the couch, tenses up.

In English, D'Aubuisson says, slowly.

"Would you repeat the question?"

"Why did you kill Archbishop Romero?"

Someone inhales. There's some murmuring. They hold each others' eyes.

D'Aubuisson leans forward, and with real venom, says,

"When responding to a lie like this, you have to consider the source. And as the source is American Ambassador Robert White and he is a homosexual, a Communist and an alcoholic one does not have to even answer this crazy question."

He then inclines his head at Rategan, as if to say, satisfied?

Before Rategan can answer, D'Aubuisson is swept out of the room, past the 60 minutes crew, into his Landcruiser and gone, screeching tires, dust and sirens.

60 minutes is enraged, Rowena incensed, as they push their way through the restive crowd to the car. As it speeds off, Rategan plays the clip, as she shakes her head in bewilderment.

"That was a Kamikaze stunt. He gave you an answer you can't use. Now you're a target. Happy?"

"Yep"

He had his clip. And 60 minutes had zip.

All he needs now is a new atrocity. And in the next 48 hours.

Back at the hotel he goes straight up to bed. He listens to the occasional chatter of automatics, thinking an expert would know whether they are American M16 (government forces) or AK's (guerrillas).

Staring at the ceiling, structuring the documentary in his head, he feels how lucky and happy he is and falls into a deep, exhausted sleep.

Early next morning he wakes up and pads to the bathroom. There, on the floor beneath the door, is an envelope. He opens it.

"108 asesinados. Volcan San Juan. Millas 73. Cruz Verde".

On a folded scrap of paper, in pencil.

Downstairs at six-fifteen, Sam, who doesn't have the dough to stay in the hotel and who has come from his rented room nearby, is waiting, super keen. Rategan hands him the note.

"Shit. That's where we are going. Green Cross. The guerrillas' Red Cross."

Anxious. Keeps swearing under his breath.

"Here. Fuck. No. Shit. Left here, here. Fuck, Right here. Shit no. back. Fuck. What's the time.?"

In a barrio, corrugated roofs, yapping dogs, they find the place. Knock on the tin door. From down the street, a face full of fear pops out, a teenage boy with thick hair. He waves them into the tiny Cruz Verde office. Thick with filing cabinets, piles of paper, flags. The young kid's elder brother, who runs this Cruz Verde office, sits behind a desk.. He murmurs urgently to Sam. Rategan is recording it all.

"Volcan San Juan. Massacre."

The air is crackling with something bad.

The two men are conversing hurriedly, almost in a panic.

"Pronto."

Sam brushes by him, out onto the street, the kid slams the door behind them, sliding shut bolts. They jump into the car.

"Go, go, go. Camino Major. East. Pronto."

"What the fuck was that"

"He's on a death threat, has to go underground. Lets go."

Sam is a different kind of American from the celebrity war correspondents in the bar, playing poker and drinking bourbon all night. He is seriously engaged. Rategan can't quite tell how much he is fuelled by his conscience and how much by naked ambition. But he's the best kind of American journalist. His hunger for facts, for research is bottomless. But there is something else in there that Rategan can only describe as a soft kind of righteous anger. An anger not easily quelled. He has seen it in the best of the anti-apartheid revolutionaries he had known in South Africa, of one in particular who had been found dead in a shower in prison. A man he had worked with, done meetings, travelled, gathered testimonies, printed flyers with. The liberation movement is losing the South African battle badly, but he is amazed that, here, thousands of miles away with this Midwestern American with a moustache like Errol Flynn, he is getting exactly the same buzz. As they hurtle along a bomb-damaged road, he isn't sure whether he feels dread or joy at its return.

They find milepost 73, and turn up a dirt track. There is a cattle gate. A very old man in a broken straw hat with a hole in it totters towards the car. Sam says something to him. He nods and points along two dirt tracks that disappear over a burned-out cornfield. As they drive past, Rategan sees the man's dead white eyes. He is blind. But one doesn't question his guidance.

Before them rises a volcano, a green fist into the blue sky.

They come to the remains of a village. From the logs and the ruined shacks, it looks to Rategan as if it has been burned out some time ago, not recently.

Sam yells from a gully on the other side of the path they have driven up. They leave the green car there, as the road has long since petered out into a cow track. He goes over. There's a bunch of bones piled up at the bottom of the gully.

When he gets closer Rategan gets that icy feeling down his spine. There are two skulls. Another one, baby-sized. Lots of other bones. Shit, Rategan thinks to himself, where's the forensic knowledge when you need it. Because they look to him sun-bleached, like they have been around for months, years. 108 asesinados. Not really evidence of that.

Sam is hyper-ventilating though, through either shock or like this may be his Pulitzer.

It's not about to matter anyway. Rategan hears the click before he sees it and the cold feeling in his spine shoots up again.

"Alto. Levanta las manos."

Hands up, he turns slowly. A man in regular clothes has a machine gun trained on them. A second man stands with a machete dangling. A third, a girl who looks 13 years old, stands pointing a handgun. Now the ice shoots up his cortex into his brain, rock solid fear.

"A quien?" the machine gun says.

"Nosotros periodistas. Yo, Estados Unidos."

Rategan gets in quickly

"Yo Canadiense."

At moments like these, a millisecond becomes an eternity, and Rategan thinks of running, but then immediately the volley of bullets. Naaah.

"Passaportes."

They look like guerrillas. Thin. The second guy has a bandanna around his wrist. Not escuadron del muerta, the White Hand, or Arena. No designer glasses.

"Un hombre Juan a la Cruz Verde dice nosotros a 108 asesinados a la."[10]

Rategan gestures up at the volcano. Machine gun takes their passports, and gestures for them to sit on a log while gun girl and machete man keep an eye.

After some back and forth on the walkie-talkie, Machine gun tells them they are to come with them, to their base where the Commander waits, further into the volcano. He seems relaxed and hands back their passports.

———◆———

They are held at a base camp, essentially three shacks tucked into the mountain, hidden under foliage. Sam and Rategan end up having a tactical debrief from the guerrilla's military commandante, which Rategan records, Commandante Diego (a nom de geurre, after Maradona) tells them the military cleans out smaller

---

[10] "Juan at Green Cross told us there were 108 assassination victims here"

non-combat villages and killed 8 at the one we just came through about two weeks before. Two children. War crimes, he says. The volcanoes around the capital hide many small units of guerrillas all free to strike on their own at military convoys and melt away; then show up in the city to blow up a police station or military facility. Strong clips for the doc.

It's apparent that they are not the only ones to get a note about the non-existent 108 assassinations. There are at least three other news organizations that have been tipped off. Notably a very loud CNN Washington correspondent. He is a short man, with a voice you can hear across a valley. He has a bad leg, and walks with a pronounced limp.

It is Thursday; the correspondent berates his guerrilla captors (although it has to be one of the most laid-back detentions ever) through the deeply embarrassed CNN translator.

"Tell him, and don't sugarcoat it, that I HAVE TO BE IN LONG ISLAND SATURDAY FOR A VERY IMPORTANT FAMILY WEDDING. VERY VERY IMPORTANT. DOES HE UNDERSTAND?"

The translator explains quietly to the commandante, who is leaning on a desk made out of a crate, his walkie-talkie standing on the box, various notebooks and charts spread out. He answers the translator bluntly.

"He says he wouldn't want a US-created war to interrupt your social life"

Well! CNN pops up, swears a blue streak, and storms out of the hut and starts hobbling at speed towards the valley below. The armed guards, heretofore dozing in the heat, spring out of their hammocks, catch up to him and wave him back with their weapons. A veteran American UPI writer tells CNN to chill.

"No point is getting these guys all wired, man. They could run out of patience." he warns.

"PATIENCE. PATIENCE. I'M THE ONE RUNNING OUT OF FUCKING PATIENCE. I HAVE TO GET BACK TO THE HOTEL, FILE MY SHIT BY SIX AND GET ON THE NEXT PLANE HOME. I HAVE TO BE IN DC BY TOMORROW NIGHT. I HAVE TO BE IN LONG ISLAND BY SATURDAY. NOT STUCK HERE WITH MY FUCKING LIFE IN THE HANDS OF THESE FUCKING JERKS."

At that, all of us, detainer and detainee alike, stare at this pop-eyed twat.

"IT'S MY NIECE'S FUCKIN WEDDING FOR CHRISSAKES."

It's a brief moment but Rategan is convinced that none of them would have raised a finger if he'd been shot right there. Just a calf or arm job, just to make him squeal, and put family weddings into perspective. He would be a star turn at the reception, bandaged and boasting.

The walkie-talkie eventually squawks into life, the armed guys come half to attention, orders are rapped out from someone somewhere, and they are on their way back down the mountain, past the singed village of three skulls, and to the car. Except for the CNN star, who is picked off the volcano by a chopper.

They never did find the mass grave with 108 assassination victims. But they did get back to the hotel in one piece before curfew.

They are decompressing with a beer when Sam says

"Uh-oh"

Fermin is back, looking very anxious.

"The morgue" he says.

Sam and Rategan sit in the back of the green Toyota, slumped, beer on their breath, no food in them, both wearing shades, dreading what's coming.

The morgue is a low concrete bunker. Outside, Goats chew the uncut grass. Rategan records ambience.

The boss has left so they slip the guard a few dollars.

There on a concrete slab lie the two bodies.

Joaquin the Cruz Verde contact has taken one right in
the forehead. His dead hands are still bound behind him.

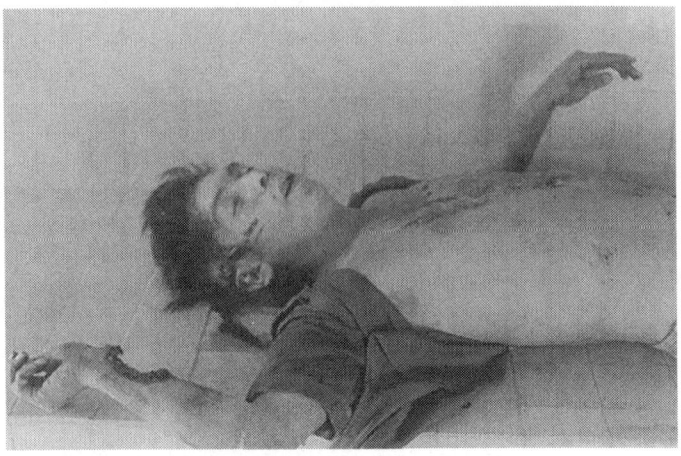

His younger brother has half his skull blown away, the
thick hair exploded away from the shot, and his arm is
frozen in a gesture intended to stop the bullet that ended
his life. Along the boy's arm, right where the bullet flew,
a half-moon cavity wound.

That's what you do to try and protect yourself, Rategan
thought.

Of course you would do that. It's a perfect half moon,
slightly torn on the inner side.

Rategan, on automatic, appalled for a millisecond at
himself, slowly gets out his Pentax camera and takes
a shot.

He also records the morgue ambience: to be mixed behind a script he shall write and record later.

He records the ambient sound of two dead bodies on a cement slab in a Central American morgue.

He has seen the dead before and he would see dead bodies again but he will never forget these two. Joaquin's teenage brother and the way he lies in death. The pathetic, instinctual self-defence of that arm. And is it because they had told the press about a massacre that may not have even happened?

This is the moment Rategan chooses sides in the Salvadorean war.

Back in the hotel bar, by the third rum, the rage has surged up his chest and is gnawing at his throat. He knows himself well enough to know that it is time to remove himself from the company of others. The red mist is seeping over his vision. He knows that if he doesn't get out right then, away from the American crews swapping jokes about the bang- bang they had shot that day, away from the loud-mouthed South African yappity-yapping about all the action he has seen, he will hit somebody hard. It's happened before. Move on, move on.

Sam is deeply affected too, and the best Rategan can do is embrace him in the parking lot, before he goes up to his room. There he tears his clothes off and throws himself on the bed. He is behind schedule on the doc. There are multiple messages from Toronto.

Within a minute, he is asleep.

Rategan hears a soft knock on the door. It's just after midnight. He drops noiselessly out of bed, and through the eyehole catches somebody heading off down the corridor. He opens and sees Rowena the NY Times woman. She is dressed in a coat over pajamas, and slippers.

She comes inside and stands very close. He feels his body reacting. She pushes him back onto the bed, opens her gown and slides down onto him. They gasp with the shock, the heat of contact. She thrusts her hips onto him with fierceness, grinding strongly, digging her fingers into his side, suppressing noises until they sound like sobs. There is a lot of other stuff going in inside her. She is doing this through some desperation, through rage at someone else. In an explosion of gagged fury, it is over, she slumps down onto him and he feels her heat and sweat and tears, the wetness of her face on his cheek. He puts his hands on the back of her head and turns it towards him, but she resists and rolls away. She lets herself out. They haven't exchanged a word, and she will never come again.

About two-thirty ayem he's awakened again. He's been dreaming of the younger brother trying to say something, but his face twists away.

Rategan is aware of a surreal sense of rocking. The rocking is almost maternal. His eyes open slowly. The room is swaying. Gently, but definitely swaying!! At the end of each sway, there is a click. Rategan thinks "Earthquake"

The click, he thinks, is the sound of reinforcing steel rods snapping in the cement walls. Holy Shit. Holy, holy shit. An earthquake. Twenty-third floor. If this thing comes down, he goes down in the rubble. Shit.

He is seeing his Mother in South Africa and how devastated she will be, when she gets the news about her boy dying in an earthquake in a Central American country she's barely heard of. This image, her horrified face, and the ice in the spine again, before he swings slowly out of bed with the sway.

It settles. He can hear sirens, some alarms, shouting. He is so tired, from the killings, the rum, the sex and now this.

He will not run. The elevators or stairs will crush or trap him.

He grabs his tape recorder and pads across to the windows. It seems most of the street lamps have gone out, but other lights are flashing. An ambulance flashes by on the street below. There is another tremor, not a rocking one this time, more like an after-shiver from deep below.

All he can think of doing is turning on his tape recorder. He manipulates the cantilevered windows so that the microphone is wedged tightly, pointing out into the night. Everything is still now. Aftermath silence. He thinks of all those images he has seen over the years of collapsed buildings after earthquakes.

It's an act of God. He accepts God's Will. If the CBC finds the tape recorder in the rubble, maybe they can use the sound effects, and the trip wouldn't have been a complete waste of the taxpayer's money. This is what he is thinking as he pads back, gets into bed, pulls the sheet over his head and falls back to sleep, thinking how can this all be happening, back to back to back.

And when is he going to find an hour to write the doc.

He spends the day writing, isolating clips, lists, couple of long phone calls, and it is done. He gets 25 minutes out late Saturday. Everyone's happy.

His foreign editor tells him he should go off for two weeks and get behind the lines, report on the state of the battle, with access to the guerrillas critical.

He learns from Sam that if he wants to contact the guerrilla leadership he has to travel to the easternmost zones of El Salvador, to the mountainous jungles of San Miguel province. There the guerrillas control big swaths of territory.

The Military are launching a major military operation there over the next two weeks. Sam has figured out a cover, that they will go to San Miguel to do a story about a group of coffee workers demanding better working conditions.

They set out in the Green Toyota, sleeves up, windows open, another day of war in paradise. So many of the world's brutal wars take place in such beautiful places.

In San Miguel, they stay in the motel restaurant right opposite the military cuartelle in the capital, owned by a Chinaman.

"The Lucky Dragon"

Rategan pays for the rooms and his dinner and Mr. Chu figures out the change on his abacus. The solid little silver balls blur and thud into the aged wood. It reminds him of something his father had once said to him in a bank in Africa.

"A Chinaman with an abacus can figure out the numbers quicker and more accurately than the best bankers in England."

Mr. Chu's lovely Salvadorean wife is wiping glasses and replacing them behind the bar. Rategan has seen his happy little Chinese-Salvadorean kids playing in the back yard.

Jackson Browne plays softly in the background.

"How did you end up running this place at the end of the Central American Highway?" Rategan asks.

"You want to know the story, hey?"

"Sure. Why not close down, and take your family somewhere safe until the war is over?"

"You want to know this story?"

"Yeah. Give me another drink and I'll listen."

"Rum and coke?"

"As usual."

There is a suspicious-looking character at the far end of the restaurant, but he is barely within earshot, and seems absorbed in his own world.

Sam has crashed with a bad case of the runs. He is beating himself up with responsibility for Joaquin's and Joaquin's brother's deaths. Did he lead the death squad to them? He is a sweet, brilliant but dolorous Irishman from Minnesota. His conscience cuts deep.

There is a midnight-to-dawn curfew. The high security lamps from the barracks and the guard towers shed a white light across the road through the mesh of the motel bar, onto which moths and other night flyers ping and perish.

"I always wanted my own business." Chu says,

"Before I left him in China, my father said, you must own your own business otherwise you will be a slave like me. And it will kill you.

So I went to Vancouver and worked in Chinatown. When I tried to open my own restaurant they said, no, enough restaurants here already. Go south.

So I went to San Francisco and worked there. When I asked for permission and money to open my own place they said, too many restaurants here. Go south. So I did.

To San Diego. Same thing there. Mexico, the same.

So I said I will travel south on the Panamericano until there are no more Chinese restaurants. And that's how I came to San Miguel. Twenty years ago."

"Hah. Mr. Chu!"

Rategan raises his glass.

"From the bottom of my heart, I salute you."

"Hah. Thank you."

"And now with your babies, you are really stuck, huh?"

"Yes, when they grow, maybe they will go south, too"

He cackles loudly.

"Hah. No. They will be doctors and engineers."

Rategan slugs back the rest of the drink, and digs in to pay.

"No-no" Chu waves his hand. "On the house"

His wife stops wiping and looks at him, surprised.

Rategan walks off, turning through the beaded curtain that leads to his room across the yard, at the back.

He turns to Chu.

"At the end of the road YOU found the pot of gold, no?"

"We shall see. We shall see"

Later that night, Rategan awakes to the sound of loud whispers and scurrying footsteps outside his window. Then the sound of something clanking, and a harsh word, like a command.

An RPG discharges right outside his window. There is a distant thud and zing, and Rategan realizes right away what is going down. The guerrillas are launching their weekly attack on the cuartel from right outside his window.

Another Rocket.

A tremendous volley of machine gun fire pings off the roof of the motel as Rategan tumbles under the bed. In a pause between shots he hears the guerrillas hurling the RPG onto a metal surface and what sounds like a half-ton pickup screeching off into the night, with exchanges of automatic fire continuing between the neighbourhood and the military base.

Rategan stays under the bed until everything falls quiet. There is a voice at the door.

"Rategan.. Rategan.. you ok?"

"Yeah, yeah I'm fine."

A baby is crying in the background.

"Go be with your kids, Mr Chu. I'm okay."

"Okay. Keep your lights off. You get discount. See you in the morning.'

"Yeah. Good night Mr. Chu."

He will never know whether this has anything to do with the exiles he had met in Mexico, but, next morning at The Lucky Dragon, he gets a note from the guerrillas. It's directions into the mountains.

It's a much longer drive south than they expected, but eventually they come to a certain milepost, and turn down a track into the bush. They cross a riverbed beneath yet another blown-up bridge high above them. At a second milepost way up a twisting dirt road they turn up a gulch into a big, green volcano. They stash the Green Toyota in a scar in the side of the high-banked gully, and cover it with branches. A scout who looks about 12 emerges from the bushes and leads them two-thirds the way up the volcano to a company of guerrillas in a village. On the way up two more armed teenagers, fighters with mules, laden with empty water containers, pass by heading down to the river. They pause, get on their walkie-talkies and after an okay, wave them up. Soon they are met by a young woman, a very small young woman with the regulation brown gear and weapon. Soon the village emerges, less than that really, only three shacks, chickens, dogs, goats and staring children in filthy t-shirts and nothing else, with the big why in their eyes.

A large fit bearded man emerges. He is introduced as Commandante Miguel, the regional political Commandante of this brigade of the Ejercito Revolucion Partido.

Turns out he is a medical doctor from... Cuba.

Rategan recognizes two things right away. This confirms everything US President Reagan is saying about the Salvadorean uprising, that it's inspired and led by the Reds in the hemisphere, even better, a Cuban over a Nicaraguan. The second thought Rategan has is that this guy is straight out of central casting. Barrel- chested, bearded, dark-eyed, open-shirted, rumble-voiced, decisive, analytical and completely in charge, fluent in English, as well as a committed patria-o-muerte capable of dealing it out and dying gloriously. He resembles Franco Harris, the Pittsburgh Steelers running back. Rategan, in that perverse way that shoots through him unpredictably and at any moment in time and place, is chilled by the flash of a Guevara/Biko death mask behind the full-of-life face.

Women fighters stand around in their bush fatigues, each one wearing something red. A bandanna, a wrist rag, a red piece of cloth around their Kalashnikovs. Beautiful, young women from poverty- ravaged rural villages and coffee plantations; probably some middle-class kids from the university campuses, which have been closed down in this region after a series of lethally-suppressed protests. The Salvadorean military guns down students with even more violence than the South Africans.

Sam's requests-through-intermediaries have reached this group and they have agreed to let them travel with them for a few days to get first-hand reports of the war, inside the guerrilla's experience of it.

Sensational, thinks Rategan.

Right away they agree to give an interview. Commandante Miguel slides a log under him and sits down.

"Comencemos. Primero pregunta."

He gives his nom-de-guerre, He is originally from Santiago-de-Cuba, a doctor who has done post-graduate medical training in Mexico City.

He gives a comprehensive analysis of the conditions on the ground, the strike-and-retreat tactics, the constant moving through the mountains. He then spools back through history, with reference to the exploitation of coffee and cotton farmers by the oligarchs, the quatorze familias who control 87% of the wealth of El Salvador. Finally he places it all in the context of the strategic battle for the Americas. He's brilliant. After 15 minutes Rategan has more than he can use.

20 minutes in, one of the women behind him snaps her fingers and they all quieten. She points a finger skyward. Miguel puts his fingers to his lips. The faint sound of a plane in the sky. In recent weeks there had been reports that the CIA is using light planes to track guerrilla movement and transfer the locations to the Salvadorean military on the ground. This is a step beyond the congressional mandate, technically illegal. Sure enough, a goddamn small plane can now be distinctly heard coming from the east, getting closer and more distinct.

"Salir!" One word.

Sam and he included. Leave.

As he swings his weapon over his shoulder the Cuban demands, aggressively.

"Were you followed? Suddenly he is looking distinctly hostile.

They shrug.

"You must go. Now"

Suddenly they are all gone, melting into the bush in a matter of minutes.

Rategan blinks at Sam as if it was a mirage. There's a beat or two of stunned silence, the plane clearly visible above them now, banking. As one they start down for the car, trying to stay under the overhanging foliage. Above them they can clearly see the wing markings of the plane, encircling the side of the volcano. They can almost see the sun reflecting off the pilot's glasses.

Suddenly the sound of automatic gunfire... from below. At first they break into a run. A second burst. They look at each other. Fear and panic surges through Rategan and he remembers The New York Timer's advice "never get caught between the lines"

They burst into a gallop down the gully, between earthen banks above shoulder height. A third burst closer, a human whelp and a strange squealing bray.

"They shot the mule"

One of the young men that had passed them on the way down, comes scrambling up the path.

"Que pas?"

"Soldados." And on he goes, eyes wide with terror.

Sam and Rategan pause.

"Let's tell'em we're journalists, but lets move"

They break into a run yelling out "Periodista, periodista" against the hail of bullets they expect at any millisecond. They both realize how ludicrous it sounds. Sam tears the branches off the roof and piles in. Rategan backs up and wrenches the steering wheel out into the gully. They hurtle down the gulch, banging off the walls and fishtail out onto the dirt road, barely short of the cliff on the other side and swivel downhill, right, at speed. There, facing them, about 50 yards away, a company of soldiers, weapons ready. They skid to a halt. Rategan flips the cassette with the Cuban's interview on it out of the recorder and into his sock, flipping in the spare he always keeps back into the Sony.

Sam is staring fixedly at the approaching sergeant, looking white as a sheet. Rategan is ready to be torn apart, but he finds, in himself, a memory of how he greeted the Chief of the South African Defence Force at Speech Day at his old school.

He smiles as the man approaches, accompanied by two weapon-wielding subordinates.

"Buenos Dies Colonel" any rank in a crisis.

The officer scrutinizes the Prensa International sign on the dash. I hope to fuck he's read the Geneva Convention, Rategan thinks.

"Periodistas" says Sam.

"Nosotros. We are researching a story on how the war is affecting coffee farmers in the province."

"Have you been with the guerrillas?" the man asks from behind his shades, in Americanized English. He is sweating from the march and whatever his troop just did to the two scouts and the mule. He is glancing into the volcano from whence Rategan and Sam had spurted.

"Guerrillas? No. No"

Rategan pops the cassette out.

"Here. It's just campesinos. Nada"

And then in an instinctive act, Rategan tosses the cassette into the ravine. The sergeant's head snaps around as he follows it spiralling into the depths below.

The Colonel peers at Rategan, puzzled, impatient. These two are not the objective.. and waves them on, angrily. He is close to his quarry, and they aren't it. Unlike some of his peers, he doesn't want to waste any bullets on gringo journos.

Rategan accelerates away in a cloud of muchas graciases, past the wide-eyed soldiers. Around the first corner the dead mule, its legs sticking up from the ditch. And further on the second scout, the boy who had passed them earlier, lies there too, his body broken into the base of a bush.

They gun it down the mountain, realizing they will never make San Miguel by midnight curfew, especially since they have to find that river crossing beneath the blown out bridge in the dark. An hour later, the sun is going down through their dust trail as they whip along, and it is only the last minute glimpse of a low concrete barrier that makes Rategan slam on the brakes, inches from tumbling into the river far below.

Next day, Doyle has to head back to the capital. Rategan spends the morning at the motel, cutting and writing. He decides he is going to take the afternoon off. He needs a complete break.

He grabs a towel, and heads for the beach.

About half an hour out of town he realizes he is breaking another one of the NY Times's guy's cardinal rules of war correspondency:

"Never Travel Alone."

But hell, he is 28, has a hot green Toyota that goes like a challenger for the Roof of Africa Rally, and he is feeling light and lucky.

It is a beautiful afternoon in El Salvador, blue skies and small scudding clouds. Nature oblivious to the agonies of war. The Pacific is less than an hour south. He comes to a bridge. This one has been blown up too, but alongside the military has thrown up another makeshift crossing of barrels and planks, which they are guarding with a dozen soldiers. They poke around his car a bit. He presses 100 googoos on the guy in charge, and explains he just wants to go for a swim in the sea, take a break from this Guerra; they shake their heads and wave him through. About fifteen minutes after that, he clears a rise and there it is; from one side to the other right across his windscreen, the Oceania Pacifico. Peace Ocean. Spectacular. Volcanoes to the left and behind, plains to either side, leading broadly down to the surf-lined sea.

On the road in front of him, on his side, three figures. In fatigues. They turn and face him as he approaches. As he draws closer he sees they are armed. One steps into the road. Uh-oh. He stops. Rule number one, broken again.

Never Cross Lines.

Tough to get a swim in a war zone. What are they? Escuadron del Meurte? Military? Guerrillas? Hunters?

He makes sure they see the Prensa Internationale sign, grabbing it and shaking it. But these three, two guys and a girl, seem awfully relaxed. They smile and greet him politely.

"Periodista?"

"Si."

"Que Pais?"

"Canadiense"

"A Donde va?"

"Nadar en el oceano"

They laugh.

"Porque?.. es peligroso."

He is tired and relaxed at the same time.

"Si si. Muchas Tiburon Reagan"

This they like.

"Se llama?"

"Rategan. CBC."

"Momentito"

The young man in charge walks off a ways and talks into a walkie-talkie.

"Bueno, companero. En este pueblito, informe a Commandante Ernesto. Vayos despacio, favor.... Gracias, muchas.. De Nada."

Rategan can only marvel at the bizarre nature of this war. How, over one hill one can be with the military, over the next, with guerrillas, and back by curfew. But he has no idea the big break about to come his way.

As he drives into the village plaza of La Cuca he is stunned. There are more than a hundred guerrillas there, in various states of relaxation. In civilian clothes, campesino clothes, with red bandannas, armbands and berets, most armed with shoulder weapons. A few have banderilleros of bullets draped over their shoulders. From their body language and the dust up to their knees, they look tired, like they are resting after a long march.

It reminds him what Sam had told him. An American military expert had complained than the guerrillas in these mountainous zones cover two miles for every mile the Salvadorean army cover. They are mostly country people, in their element, moving through countryside they had grown up in, many of them third generation. Years of back-breaking work building homes and stone walls, tending goats, fields of coffee, or hauling water, wood, cotton, and plantains up and down these serrated ridges. This assemblage before him is the BRAZ or Brigada Rafael Arce Zablah, named after an economics student who had been gunned down by the Army during an attack on an army post in nearby La Union in 1975. And there are a lot of them around eastern El Salvador, thirty-thousand, according to a US military source. Six combat battalions of 5000 each, trained by former Army officers. Defectors, now guerrilla combatants.

A couple of armed fighters emerge from one group and wave him like parking lot attendants to a spot under some palm trees to one side. Take down his license plate number.

They order him to follow them to a cantina, and wait. He lights a cigarette and is aware of emitting very relaxed vibes, taking his lead from the guerrillas laughing and talking outside. Laughter tinkles in the room, and in the back a dark-haired woman animatedly talks to two guerrillas. She is wearing a red u- shaped top, her hair bunched up and in sweaty streaks straggling down her neck, earrings and lots of necklaces and arm bangles.

She is very attractive and nicely drunk, happy drunk, bubbling with yap and laughter. His kinda drinker, he thinks. Oh well, not here, not now. A fighter slips back down some wooden steps and beckons. He follows.

The second floor is a large room, wooden floorboards, a large table at one end next to a large window, the silhouette of a man in deep conversation with two guerrillas, a man with long hair and an air of authority. Rategan stands there, waiting. The man finishes his conversation, and turns his attention to Rategan.

"Senor"

"Si"

"Periodista Canadiense?"

"Exacto"

"Bueno. Take a seat."

His English is good. This is always a relief as translating and recording foreign language interviews adds hours to the production of a radio doc.

Rategan explains his job and asks for an interview.

The man sticks two fingers in the air between them. He looks about 26, thinks Rategan, long brown hair, soft eyes, a slight scar on his throat, red and yellow kerchief around his neck and studs and red stars on his epaullette and breast pocket. Black beret with a rifle and machete. A tattoo on the back of his left wrist. The outline of a man with a gun and a banner.

"On two conditions."

"Yes?"

"One. This meeting never took place. Yo No Existo. And Two. You do a favour to me."

"Yes to the first. What's the favour?"

"I tell you after."

"OK."

Trust.

The man readies himself.

"I too have a favour."

"Uh-uh?"

"After the interview I'd like to go for a swim in the sea, here."

He laughs, and nods.

"Como no?"

Rategan pulls his Sony tape recorder out of his bag, its black leather casing covered in a fine layer of golden dust, plonks it on the table, checks the juice, plugs in the mike, pauses.

"It's about three o clock. I'd like to interview you for twenty minutes or so, an analysis of the war right now. Then, the swim. Then I have to drive back to San Miguel before curfew."

"De Nada."

"What shall I call you?"

"Commandante Ernesto. I am the military commander of the Rafael Arce Brigade. We have just got into the village after a two month operation in the mountains."

"How's that going?"

"Very well. We can move in these mountains at will. Although there has been a new development with US aid to the military from the sky, they still cannot catch up to us."

"Why not?"

"This is our territory, many of our comrades are from these hills and valleys. To you it may look very rough, but these people are used to that. Many of the government soldiers are new recruits. They have joined out of economic desperation. Our fighters are like mountain goats. Their fighters are frightened puppies. And their hearts are not in it. We are fighting for our country, for the people, Patria o Muetre. They are fighting for the oligarchs and Ronald Reagan."

"Patria o Muerte, from the Cubans?"

"It applies here too."

Ernesto points at Rategan's pack of Marlboros.

"Como no"

Rategan says, lighting his, then his own.

"How did you get into this, being a guerrilla fighter?"

"I was a second year economics student at University, in La Union. Rafael Arce was my tutorial leader! He was a brilliant thinker, an analyst, not a fighter. He was very brave, very charismatic. He led our protests, a strike at the University, over fees and impossible fees for the children of campesinos. Economic demands. A Man of Peace. He was detained and killed by the Army. We fight under his name. He was a great patriot who believed in economic equality for all Salvadoreans."

This physically weary, but intellectually disciplined ex economics student answers all Rategan's questions, his aggressive, politically hungry questions, with absolute patience and precision in good conversational English. Back and forth. The best interviews are like that, a spoon overflowing, rhythm and truth, a dance, and he will later remember this one as one of the three best he's done. Hundreds of interviews are dead compared to this.

Ernesto, 26 years old, going on 40. He leads thousands of men and women, and has sustained and inflicted as much death as anyone on the continent.

Rategan asks him about that, because the baby face is contradicted by the deep lines around the eyes.

"I have a wife who I never see. I hope if I am lucky enough to see her, I can remember how to love. War can kill this in you, however just the cause. To tell you the truth, sometimes I think this conflict has crushed the humanity in me."

There are many of these, answers to questions that Rategan knows are way outside the lives of his listeners, beyond the world of the farmer's wife driving to church outside of Fort Qu'Appelle, Saskatchewan, or the fisherman's boy in Bonavista Bay, but he is doing this as he always has, killing two searches with one microphone. After it's gone out on air, maybe the farmer's wife will shake her head in amazement or the fisherman's boy will tell his Dad.

If it is true, if he is hitting the truth vein, he believes anyone with the heart to listen and an inquisitive brain will hear and understand. And act accordingly, in their own way. It's the best he can do.

An hour has passed in the lowering sun. The interview yields to the swim. He remembers the swim quite clearly because of the Pig. Under the cantina he strips among wooden stilts that stand over the waterline, in a muddy area that acts as a sty for a mud-encrusted pig with berryblack eyes. It wallows and snorts in the shallows next to him. This is disgusting at a level that emerges in dreams years later mingled with flashes of light speeding by and nightmares of death squads in black-windowed SUV's. Yes, it's Orwell and Lennon and the Pigs.

He emerges from under the pig shack, his toes sinking into the brown volcanic sand and down into the languid warm lazy waves of the Pacific. Fifty strokes out, he breaks the salt water, rubs it from his eyes, looks out to the horizon, rotates onto his back, looks back at the cantina, the figures of guerrillas milling in the zocalo, the window behind which Ernesto runs his war.

Let's hope if I am lucky enough to see her, I can remember how to love.

Rategan rolls again into the rest of his strokes, his mind yielding to the special world he inhabits when swimming. It seems to him the closer to his truth he gets, the higher the occurrence of these starbursts of ecstasy, bursting from the seabed of freedom. He dips beneath the surface, always able to hold his breath for two full minutes, swims down, down, until it's dark, and hears it. This heartbeat beating inside himself and beneath these worlds he swims through. Africa, Caribbean, Canada, now Salvador. The Saviour. Bloodied land.

When he gets back to the muddied sty among the stilts his cassette recorder case and his clothes are still there. He changes and with no towel, still wet, goes back into the cantina, his clothes sticking to his body. While he waits for Ernesto to come down, he sees she is still there, the beauty at the back, like Isabella in Hemingway's war, or a feckless beauty in a Goya painting, arguing with two guerrillas while she throats glasses of sangria. She has silver bangles that clink and she's smoking. She reminds him of those drinking Canadian girls in Toronto; those Joni Mitchells at The Embassy or The Pilot,

"... all romantics meet the same fate- cynical and drunk and boring someone in some dark café."

The sun is low in the sky and he must go. On cue, Ernesto appears. Both of them have to wind back up, the reporter to make San Miguel before dark, the Commandante to bivouac a thousand fighters.

The woman falls silent, expectantly.

"Now the favour," says Ernesto, gesturing with an eyebrow,

"the woman in the bar".

He has to get rid of her and get her back to San Miguel right away. Would Rategan take her?

Rategan the reporter says it is one of the few rules of his trade that you never carry things or people for one side or the other across lines.

Ernesto explains how this woman has been a wartime lover (notwithstanding the wife he has spoken of earlier, Rategan thinks), and she wants to stay with him, but he cannot allow it "under any circumstances", and certainly not in her present "condicion". Rategan shakes his head. The fighter shrugs. "Esta una favor. I understand if you cannot do it." Rategan feels this image, this image he has seen somewhere before but can't place, of a woman stunned by the concussive effects of a terrible bomb, transformed in a millisecond from dancing for the boys to reeling in pieces in the ear-tingling aftermath of carnage. He shakes his head again, this time not in denial, but in remembered damage.

He looks at Ernesto, something he's always done, the moment-of-truth, eye-to-eye, the dealbreaker.

"She's not a spy?"

He snickers.

"No."

"She's unarmed"

"Si, si."

"She's not carrying papers for you?"

"No-no."

"Of any kind? I've been arrested before, and will be again. But here, by this Army. Not on my list"

His eyes meet Rategan. He has so much more weight in his than a colonial boy from Canada.

"She's a party girl. She's fun. But very smart. Don't worry. She will take care of herself"

"Ok. If I get arrested, you will spring me, no?"

"Como no?"

"OK."

He clasps Rategan's hand, and pulls him to his chest. It has an intimacy that both alarms and liquefies. Then, militarily, he snaps his finger.

"Maria. Vamanos."

She sweeps up a carpet bag, knocks a plastic chair flying, strides past them, pinching Ernesto's cheek as she passes, a sulky moue on her lips, stops briefly.

"So I'm flying Air Canada, eh?", appraising him, dazzling smile.

And on into the dusty evening sun and towards the car. She looks like a dead ringer for someone, but he can't place it. He thanks Ernesto for the interview, but it's more than that. This is one of the few people he's ever met who he feels he could have been under different circumstances. Rategan thinks, I hope he wins this war, and gets home to his wife, and learns real love again.

Once in the car, they gun it for the ridge and San Miguel. Rategan, assessing her, asks the same security questions he has asked Ernesto and feels her out about the roadblock ahead. She is, to his relief, very war-wise, to say the least. She has the sweet aroma of sangria sweat, her hair is stuck to the side of her cheeks, her bangles tinkling, and he gets it. Genevieve. Genevieve Bujold; the Quebecoise actress. She's a dead ringer for Genevieve Bujold. But this is no fucking movie, he admonishes himself. They slew over the last hillock and down to the bridge, now a fully staffed military roadblock. It looks like the division that's been chasing the Rafael Arce Bridge has camped here for the night.

They skid to a halt in front of their pointed US weapons in a cloud of dust. A soldier, as tired looking as the guerrillas they'd just left, maybe dangerously tired, schleps over to the passenger side as Genevieve rolls down the window.

On recognizing her, his expression changes to joy. He turns and yells "Maria. Maria es aqui" and soldiers come piling down from the ridge in a slide of stones and dust. Maria has pulled from her patch-coloured campesino bag a big ball of newspaper, and unfurls it to reveal, in an eruption of powerful scent, some of the richest, darkest marijuana Rategan has ever seen. Paralysis turns to relief, as he watches the soldiers grab fistfuls of marijuana from "Maria's" gypsy lap, grinning broadly at him, yelling Maria Maria Mariiaaaa (say it once and it's almost like praying) and she's suddenly urging him to

"drive drive drive

letsgethefuckouttahere,"

slapping the soldiers grasping wrists "BASTA BASTA BASTA!". Marijuana spraying everywhere, and him gunning the green Toyota rental, and the soldiers falling back, waving their guns high in the rear view mirror, letting off some rounds and blowing kisses to St Maria of Marijuana.

For some 500 yards, he drives white knuckle, processing. Then he turns to her. She has an impish smile. He shakes his head. He has some great music, he always travels with it, bangs Van Morrison's "Hard Nose the Highway" into the cassette slot. After an affirmative exchange, she rolls up a fat joint and they rock into San Miguel, feeling safer in a town.

From the dark end of the street

To the bright side of the road

We'll be lovers once again

On the bright side of the road

"I need food" she yells, as the sun dies over the cathedral. "What do you like??"

"Oysters as big as my hand." He laughs.

"No problem."

She guides him to a small shack with corrugated iron walls and a palm thatch roof where they serve oysters as big as a hand and straight liquor like cane spirit from Natal. The server greets Maria like a long lost sister. A man comes in looking a lot, to Rategan, like an off- duty military officer, also very happy to see Maria.

His mind is spinning now.

Which side is this crazy dame on??

Driving away from the oyster shack he says,

"Maria, you are amazing, but..... what side are you on?"

"We live in dangerous times. Every Salvadorean figures a way to survive this war, or not. This my way."

"What's that?"

"This is just between us."

"You can trust me."

"Ok. I will. Life is too short."

She kicks off her sandals, slides the seat back and puts one toe-ringed foot on the dashboard, the other dangling out the window, the breeze making her eyes narrow and her hair fly.

"I love Ernesto. I go and sleep with him for one or two nights when I can meet up with him. But he is an honourable man and will go back to his little village wife after the war... and I... I live here in San Miguel in a free townhouse. Very nice. I am the mistress of the owner of the townhouse. He's a pilot for the El Salvador Air Force. I am his mistress," she repeats. "He too is married."

She glances over to Rategan, gesturing with her hand

"Izquierda aqui."Then, with sudden, profound fatigue in her voice,

"It's very complicated. His wife and kids are in Florida. He is always flying US dollars to Miami for the oligarchs and the military leadership. You should do a story on that."

"What's your name?"

She looks away from him towards the road.

"My name is Maria de Los Angeles. What is your story exactly?"

He plays for time, processing the network of sex and treachery in her answers. Then decides to give her the short version.

"I'm from Toronto, Canada. The Canadian Broadcasting Corporation sent me here to do a radio documentary on the guerrillas"

"Okay."

They are heading into the heart of the city. She is thinking. He catches a glimpse of her hardening eyes. Rain clouds have gathered overhead.

"Whhaddya think so far," she says.

"I see lots of reasons to rise up. Poverty. Racism. Hunger. No work. Brutal repression. Same as every war I've covered. Too much poverty, too little freedom, clearly worth risking all to change things."

She nods. "Now that Reagan and America are behind the oligarchs, we're fucked."

He catches the steel in her voice, just then.

"We are fucked?"

He sees her glancing in the rear view mirrors, side and front.

"Left here."

She directs him to the back of what looks like an abandoned institutional building of some kind. The walls, barely visible in the evening light, have big smears of blackness.

They conceal the car behind three big crates.

She puts her hand on his arm as he puts the gear in neutral. Her sun-steeped skin is brown and hot, the bangles clink dully.

"I trust you. You must trust me. This is safe. But you cannot tell anyone about where this place is"

He nods.

She abruptly exits the car. He has to half-run to fall in behind her. She has the ass of a dancer or a Levi's model, but he quickly squelches the thought.

"Pay attention," he thinks to himself.

This is the quick and the dead here. It's a feel he's developed from who knows where. That this is the kind of place that could very suddenly erupt, and thunk, the jaw stupidly on the concrete floor, and a world dislocated with the faraway throb. Can't move.

Doesn't happen. Yet.

They speedwalk for quite a distance along an arched corridor where monks or torturers have trod, he's not sure. It's now raining torrentially, fat drops slapping down. There are weird creaks, toads croaking, dogs barking somewhere in the middle distance. She descends on three slippery concrete steps, the edges worn round by decades of feet, through a big wet wooden door. Stops. Whistles three times. There's a sound. A door opens in the darkness. They go in. A peasant woman embraces Maria sleepily.

Maria talks to the woman about him. She is nodding sweetly, but her hard eyes appraise him very seriously. She asks some questions. Then she nods. She sparks a light under a pot.

Maria say "This is Commandante Estrella. She is the urban commandante for the FMLN in this city. She is making us coffee. You can interview her, but we must be gone in 10 minutes."

Commandante Estrella murmurs.

Maria leans forward. "How do you take your coffee?"

He does a perfect five question interview. At the beginning of every answer, she says "Etonses." It's a Salvadorean expression.

"So then".

The campaneros, she says, move through the city at will, attack the military bases nightly, and melt away.

Three of the town's 8 neighbourhoods are under FMLN control. Their tactics are keeping the Army pinned down here, curtailing their ability to strike their comrades in the countryside. But more materiel, and now air surveillance is coming in from the Americans. And the Death Squads are in high gear, just like in the capital.

She then says the same thing guerrilla fighters say the world over. "We are winning the war for the hearts and minds of the masses."

There is something stoical engraved into her face, as if the price is getting too high, as if she herself has paid in children or family.

Her logic and exactitude is impressive, this face he has seen in a dozen markets in Mexico and Central America, the brown face, the black hair, the slightly angled brown eyes with the patience and indestructibility forged from centuries resisting and surviving brutality, from the Mayan years all the way down to Reagan's death squads. Genetic tenacity.

After the interview Rategan and Maria travel back through darkened, curfew streets.

She takes him to the townhouse in the suburb next to the military headquarters, and the car stops outside. She invites him inside. He declines.

"I have a girl in Canada." The shards of glass rustle, what's left of his heart.

"I will never see you again" he murmurs.

He holds her tenderly for a while feeling the heat through the straps on her damp back before she goes, this body with its enemy lovers.

On his short drive back to the Lucky Dragon, he thinks she is most likely to survive this war. Or maybe not.

He shakes his head at his day, a day like so many others in his charmed life and career. Writing in the morning, the military, Ernesto and the guerrillas, the swim, Maria de Los Angeles. What a crazy war this is. What a beautiful country. Lovely people. And the work.

There's a half-moon above the Cuartelle. It reminds him of the shape of the wound in the arm of the dead boy. Tears and terror, and a half-moon above the Cuartelle.

He thinks of all the material he has recorded on those tiny acetate ribbons in his bag, and the blades start up in his editor's brain. Start with this sound, this scene, these clips, the end.

Have Doc. Time to turn for Canada.

Drive back, drop off car, pay hotel, grab plane.

Home.

3 RATEGAN DOES GRENADA

On May 9 1992, a brand new US Air Force Bell chopper burps its lethal contents into the crest of the Grenadian hills at the rate of 600 rounds a second.

Rategan sees the silent puff and hears the delayed crackling over the uniformed shoulder of a USAF Public Affairs officer briefing the world's media at Pearl airport two-and-a-half thousand feet below.

As the cameras whirr and shutters click, the PA officer says,

"We are still mopping up Marxist guerrillas in the hills, but we do not expect any further serious resistance at this point."

"What about the Cubans?" the reporters, mostly American and British, yell.

"There are unconfirmed reports of remnants of Marxist fighters…."

To the US military-industrial spin machine, Rategan, in this group, is of very minor importance. To them, Canada is strictly second division, with no horse in the race, and, as he's only radio, he's bumped further down the ladder. An advantage, he thinks, as he backs away from the scrum, and strolls slowly towards a trio of well-worn cars, beyond the shaded gaze of the heavily armed and camo-ed military guards.

When did soldiers start wearing designer shades? An image of Patton snaps in and out. Maybe he started it. Or at least the George C Scott version.

Under a big soursop tree, behind the wheel of a dilapidated yellow Datsun, a bony, bearded dude with dreads scrutinizes him warily.

"Can you get me up there, to the hills," Rategan points, showing him three US twenties. He nods to the back but Rategan gets in the front, glancing to see that the media scrum is still firing its softballs at the US army.
They had been flown onto the island from Barbados for one hour only, "owing to the threat of Marxist terrorists and Cuban mercenaries". They will be restricted to the airport area and flown back to Barbados on the transport plane that had brought them. Back in time to get to their hotels, cut their items, and get them on the bird in time for the 1830 newscasts, Rather, Jennings and Brokaw. Then,
"Where are we eating?"

Once Ricky the driver and Rategan clear the airport, there is the odd sign of violation. Not so much of an invasion, but of normal routine snapped off here and there for a few terrifying, omnipotent minutes.
A telegraph pole snapped in two, a roof with a hole in it. At the turn of a descending hairpin road a couple

of US soldiers stand laconic guard over a car that has ditched. As they slow, Rategan notices bullet holes in a windscreen and blood on a rag, draped over the driver's headrest.

Ricky has some kind of a sticker on his windshield, which gets them through with a wave.

A general store emerges on the left.

"Whoa," Rategan cries. "Wanna patty?"

"Sure, man,"

"Which one?"

"Beef. Hot."

Rategan hasn't eaten or drunk since pre-dawn Barbados. He goes in. An Asian shopkeeper is listening patiently to an enraged Hispanic, barrel-chested, thick curly black hair.

When Rategan comes up behind them, the man whirls like a hunted animal, and blows by him, carrying a bag with bottles in it.

"Cuban all a-panic" says a woman shopper.

The man behind the counter looks at him with a can-I-help-you nod.

"Gimme two of 'em beef patties and two bottles of water, chief."

The shopkeeper turns to a heating drawer, slips tongs into the case and slides two patties into a paper packet.

Back in the car, Rasta Ricky is grateful.

Gesturing to the disappearing dust trial of a four-wheel drive, he observes, "Cuban red hot, man."

"Some lef' behind and dere not enoff Rum in Moola's store for dem skaired Cubans."

"Let's get up to the ridge, man."

"Dread."

The West Indies, Rategan remembers from a combination of history lessons, the novels of Jean Rhys and his own seafaring days here, are dotted with buildings like the one that stands before them as a silhouette on the horizon. Remnants of Colonial days.

The Morne Genoux, three stories high, faux Greco-Roman pillars, a transplanted English country mansion at the end of a three-hundred yard gravel driveway fringed by what had been topiared trees in the shape of animals, now oddly misshapen. Unbalanced giant rabbits, pheasants with beaks leaning over onto the abandoned grass.

A trio of American soldiers lolls at a guard-hut. They don't move; don't seem remotely alarmed as Rasta Ricky draws to a stop. Rategan gets out twenty yards away so they can read his body language. They seem disinterested, unfocussed.
After a wait, he approaches them.

"Hey," Rategan says.

A black soldier lazily moves his weapon off his shoulder to dangle in his arms.

"Who y'all."

"I'm the Canadian Broadcasting Corporation"

"Canada, huh?"

"Yep.."

There is something off about these boys, confirmed when they.. giggle. Comical, with the faux vegetation springing out of their helmets, and black face-paint.

"So…what's going on?" Rategan asks.

"You tell me, Canada."

"Well. I've just been told that you are encountering resistance from Marxist and Cuban guerrillas. In these hills."

"Huh?"

They started giggling, like kids on angel dust. They are high all right. High as the trash vultures that circle above.

Suddenly a Huey appears from the southeast, screams overhead, flattening the grasses. Rategan ducks. A dust fleck from a chopper can blind you. The soldiers just stand there, as if insensate, letting the chopper wash flatten the stalks on their helmets, eyes bulging from the pressure.

As the grasses fall back and the machine howls over a ridge, Rategan pulls out the international currency of confidence between correspondent and soldier. Red Marlboros. Four of the five pull one.

"Where are you guys from?"

"Pittsburgh," says the black kid, handing the packet back. Nodding appreciation.

"Keep it," Rategan says.

"Savannah, Gee-orgia" says a rangy white kid.

"Texas," said the other.

"Whereabouts?"

"Whowannaknow, Texas."

This really creases them up.

"Wherethefuck, Arkansas."

More snorts and chuckles.

A little snatch of Apocalypse Now.

Knowing these boys are not allowed to say anything other than name, rank, number and origin, he persists,

"So what went down here??"

"Listen, man, we just dropped in overnight, haven't heard or seen a thing."

"Goats and dawgs," said the black soldier.

"No resistance, contact?"

"No-thing. Zip"

"The dawgs bark in Spanish"

"Must be Cubans" They guffaw and high-five each other.

A walkie-talkie squawks. Savannah boy deals with it. Rategan hears

"Some journalist from Canada, sir."

He flips it down on his belt.

"Listen," thumbing the walkie-talkie,

"Sarge says we can't say anything. You have to contact public affairs."

"Okay" Rategan says.
"Thanks a lot."
"Yes sir."

They hear the rumble and see the C-130 banking towards Barbados, the return flight for all the international media.

"One more thing, if you don't mind?"
"Shoot."
"Do you know where you are? Who you are fighting here?"
"No man. Listen we practice this shit all the time. 82nd Airborne. Middle of the night, up we go, drop in, ready for whatever. Not a damn thing. Real disappointin'"
"Ready for a fight, man. Sweet fuck all."
The black guy laughs again, speedy.
"You're in Grenada. Fighting the New Jewel Movement." says Rategan
"Huh?"
"Whatever, dude. Nobody got killed"
"Yet." says the Texan.

He's been here before. To the islands. 21 years before. He has a feel for the place, the people. He likes them a lot, the beautiful accents, the Caribbean version of British culture, the music.

At 19, Rategan had sailed in from the South Atlantic to Antigua, 60 days on the Atlantic, gotten a job on the good ship Mars. Dodgy trading schooner, an old Baltic Trader. Wooden. Big mast and sails. 1926 Danish engine, a Grenau. Trading lime, plastic shoes, bricks and some viscous cane liquor, many bottles of which are 'damaged' en route. Owned by Jock Davis, a Cockney Bully, a dead ringer for one of the Great Train Robbery characters.

Off Roseau, in Dominica, they'd unloaded a few crates, and dropped anchor about two hundred yards from the seawall. The boys go ashore. Elim, Gaso and Rategan. There's a bar down by the river that's open, a corrugated iron shack with a juke. A fridge, Carib beer, rum and some skinny looking skanks in torn t-shirts. Marley singing "Please Don't Rock My Boat". Reggae's early days.

They sit there talking and drinking in the sun. Women wash clothes in the river, which looks pretty skuzzy. All is calm.

As it gets dark, they stroll back towards the dock to another spot, a little more upmarket, with an actual sign, and a nice wooden bar, stools and booths, and Nat King Cole. They drink some more there. They are fixing to leave when Gaso gets into a spat with an Espanol. He calls him something, something the man doesn't like. There's a lot of slang Rategan can't keep up with. But Gaso is sucking and smacking his mouth, a pre-fight tic hereabouts, Rategan has learned.

Gaso has the back and legs of an undernourished Olympic 400 meter runner, flashing chompers for teeth.

He isn't particularly good-looking but he has a tight-coiled body and attitude. Electricity pulses off him.

He is trouble waiting to happen. He has a woman in every port, and will jump anything that dances. Fights are attracted to him like mosquitos to other men.

Gaso is his nickname. Rategan wonders why. Probably because he is like gasoline-on-fire. His temper, the flame.

All the Caribbean seamen Rategan sails with have nicknames. Stanley "Old Man" Carter, 'cos he was old, Carlos "Piston" James, 'cos he is the engineer and has a body like Mr Universe. Capt. "Sea" King, 'cos he is more sea-man than hu-man. More like a Snapping Moray. And so it goes. They called Rategan "Raas", an insulting word for a white man. Translation "Arse."

Gaso is cackling 'bout "bumklaat Puerto Rican" as the three of them walk back up the village, away from the seafront bar.

Rategan, the white South African kid, Elim the mate, also 19 and the son of mean ol' Capt Sea King, and Gaso, spittin' and cacklin'. They have just had a conversation about meeting at the boat later. Elim and Gaso have girls to see. They agree not to leave with the rowboat until two ayem, so no-one will get left behind. They are getting paid eight Beewee a week and have no money to stay in Roseau.

They hear a shout, and turn.
"Hey Negro."

About sixty yards away, the Latino stands swaying under the sign. He has put on a white hat and a white jacket. He moves his hand, something glints underneath the street lamp, there is a flash, a crack, and a ping, and they fly off into the shadows.

"Negro Puta" comes the yell and two more shots.

Gaso is gone in a clatter of sheet metal and an eruption of stray dogs, as is Elim. Rategan finds an alley and hides behind a big board. And waits. He can see the man stumbling up the street to where the flood of the overhead light ends, but doesn't risk going further. He lacerates the night with racist Spanish profanities, but he runs out of conviction. Eventually after a few more "puta negros" and "fuckin' gabrons" the footsteps raggedly recede, and silence falls. Rategan lets his head drop forward and he feels his stubble rasp against his drunken chest.

He has been shot at for the first time.

He would never forget the man in the white jacket and hat under the street lamp, swaying and then...shooting. Shooting at him. How cool was that. He chuckles.

After a while Rategan hears a rat scuttle nearby and decides to crawl out from behind the board and head out of the alley.

He has a couple of hours to kill before the two ayem rendezvous.

He walks and walks, almost to the edge of town, and when he hears music, follows it. First it is Herb Alpert and the Tijuana Brass. It's a hotel with sailboats moored below in the water. In the Yacht Club bar, he meets two drinkers. They are phlegmatic Midlanders, radio engineers on an 18-month contract from Brummagem. They talk about home, Dominica, cricket. Gerry and the Pacemakers come and go, as do Herman's Hermits and more booze, which the lads seem happy to pay for. They are bored shitless, says one, and enjoy the company of this white sailor boy who has wndered out of the darkness. They invite him back to their government villa up on the hill overlooking the town, between a large crucifix and the radio tower they are installing. Rategan can see the good ship Mars at anchor in the bay below. He drinks more, but he has already drunk too much. It's getting close to two so he takes off, leaving the two Brits nodding off. They were so boring they were the kind of guys you would duck out of sight to avoid, but they had served a purpose. They had reminded him of one of the many good reasons why he was here, far away from places like Birmingham. Some of his relatives lived there, lives boring beyond the point of return.

He didn't know where the fuck *he* was going, and where all this would lead, but he did know he was moving away from that, from what had driven DH Lawrence crazy.

Salt of the Earth indeed. Thanks for winning the war, but, please, time to move on.

Now, here, under the stars in the Caribbean night, he sings to himself as he descends the dirt road to the seawall.

The boat has gone.

Elim is sitting on the dock of the bay, drunkenly asleep above the soft swell, which rises and falls into the seawall ten feet below.

Rategan nudges him awake.

"Gaso gwan tek dee bo-at, mon," he slurs. "Fuck" says Rategan. "Wha 'appen?"

Rategan picks up the patois so easy.

"After dee dago shot at oss, Gaso go sleep wid dis woman. And does 'is bizness but the woman's man come back and ketch 'em an he jomp out of window, kot 'is leg, hobble down 'ere, and wid the man an a machete runnin' and screamin' he jomp in, tak dee boat and head off. I see it all from back dere," pointing to a culvert.

Rategan stands erect and feels the onshore zephyr. Like the waves, the world is going up and down, up and down. He looks out at the good ship Mars bobbing enticingly on the calm ocean, about two hundred yards off. He can see the stern light just illuminating the soft folds of the mainsail that he'd roped earlier, and the pilot light in the cabin where his blanket and pillow lie in wait.

The gulls wheel like ghost fragments.

He's been shot at, consorted with sluts and Brits, and huddled in a pissy alley with rats. He's had enough entertainment for one night.

"Fuck it. I'm swimming."

"No man, Raas, ya drown."

"No man. It's just right *there*." Pointing at the warm, dry, safe boat.

If he slept on the seawall, right there, maybe the crazed cuckold with his machete would burst upon their sleeping bodies and slice 'em up real good. No po-lice protect-shun around here after midnight.

"No Raas, ya too drunk."

"I'm goin' man."

He takes off his shirt and pants with his wallet and passport in the pockets, and his sneakers, and rolls 'em up tight and gives them to Elim.

"You toss 'em to me."

Elim takes the bundle, reluctantly.

In his briefs and T-shirt Rategan leaps the ten feet and is sobered by the hit on the water, and then embalmed by its warm depths.

One reason to thank God, or Jah, the Caribbean Sea. What a blessed ting, mon. He treads water and turns towards the ship. It looks close enough. Back in Southern Africa, he was a strong swimmer, a record-breaker at the Highlands School Gala at the age of 11. Huh.

He waves at Elim, catches the bundle before it hits the water, and, holding it above him, starts count-swimming. He will count to 150 before looking up. When he does he sees that he is halfway between the sea wall and the boat, whose stern is pointing towards him. He does it again. 150 strokes with one arm, face into the water, mouth opening for air every three strokes, holding the bundle aloft, and dry with his left.

He stops, looks, *but the boat is no closer.* It has swung on its anchor with the shifting current and is now at least another 150 strokes *further* out. Just at that moment he swallows a huge lungful of seawater. His raised left arm now is beginning to cramp at the shoulder, the muscles behind his knees burning. He treads water furiously, looking back to see if he should head back to the seawall. Nope; that's too far.

The drunken confidence has worn off. He is officially freaked. Not for the first time, he thinks of his death at 19, a death his family back in South Africa and England would find unfathomable. One of those weird stubs in the paper.

Rategan Edwardes, schoolboy cricket prospect drowned... (wait for it*).. off the island of Dominica in the Antilles Islands of the Eastern Caribbean. No foul play suspected. Body not recovered. Memorial service, St Martins-in-the-Fields. 3 pm. Saturday.*

He can see his private school associates wrenching their faces with incomprehension.
"Where the hell *is* Domenica...and what the hell was he doing there???"
"Must have gone Native."
"Good riddance, I say"
What a waste. His mother would weep a deluge, would be destroyed. She had never wanted him to go off like he had, though it was her frustrated wanderlust, her loathing of how she had become trapped as a colonial engineer's wife, that propelled him out of doomed South Africa.

Another wavelet elbows him in the back of the head, and so he takes the deepest breath he can muster. He is now swimming underwater with his left hand just above the surface, still trying to keep the damn bundle dry.

The strangest thought comes to him.

I am not going to die a Virgin.

I am going to know a woman.

I am not going to die a Virgin.

After what seems like an eternity he breaks the surface, heaving and gasping, his whole body wracked with exhaustion, and there, like a sweetly smiling granny rocking on her stoep lies the good ship Mars, right above him.

He grasps the anchor chain and kisses it, as he regains breath. He has dodged death twice in one night. And he has never felt so alive.

More vitally, he has had a glimpse into what is really important to him.

In St George's, Grenada, Rategan needs a place to crash.

Ricky the Rasta takes him to Mrs. Brown's. He rents her room.

A nine-year old boy stares at him as he moves in. Grandson, no father. Mother a nurse in Ottawa.

He hears on BBC that the US choppers have bombed the local mental asylum.

The Richmond Hill Mental Hospital is just up the hill from Mrs. "Brung's".

There's a massive hole in its roof.

In an open courtyard a man circles, singing.
Blond Rasta dreads, skinny, in striped yellow boxer shorts.

"Home Home on the range
Where the deer and the antelope play."

In a fantastic tenor that wheels the gulls and the sky, ringin' out for all the citizens to hear.

"Where seldom is heard a discouraging word And the skies are not cloudy all day"

18 have been killed here. Most of the other 60 inmates lie in fetal positions, or wander the streets in a daze.

The US Military Public Affairs group issues a statement.

"While the Coalition reaffirms its policy of where possible not harming civilians, and it apologizes for this mistake, there was intel that Cubans and Marxist guerrillas were collecting in the surrounding area on the night in question."

> *"How long shall they kill our prophets*
> *While we stand aside and look"*
> Bob Marley

Maurice Bishop is yet another example of the prophet in Marley's "Redemption Song."

Portrayed as the "cause" of all the trouble in Grenada, he is a fascinating individual, his life story a classic of those twisted victims of colonial cruelty.

His father had worked all his days for 5 cents a week as a labourer. When the work dries up on Grenada, he moves to Aruba to work at the oil refinery, where Maurice is born.

Bishop is the most brilliant member of his generation. As a schoolboy in Grenada he aces history and is an outstanding debater. He reads law at Gray's Inn in London, travels widely in the US, East and West Germany, and Czechoslovakia. He reads prodigiously, always plotting a return to Grenada, building a network called the New Jewel Movement to help him overthrow the corrupt and brutal government of Eric Gairy. In 1979, at the age of 35, while Gairy is away at the UN, he seizes power in a coup.

Travelling to Cuba and getting support from Fidel Castro, criticising American hegemony in the region, Bishop attracts the ire of the anti-communist Reagan White House.

When Bishop has Cuban engineers extend an airport, Point Salines, Reagan sees medium range Soviet nuclear bombers minutes from the Florida coast.

But he needs a more prosaic motive. There are some American kids studying at a medical school in St

George's. The Reagan White House whips up fears for their safety, and the invasion, "Operation Urgent Fury" is unleashed, in part, to "save" them.

In advance of the landing, the Grenadian Army does the US's dirty work, taking Bishop and his circle to a Fort overlooking the harbour, and executing them. Their remains are never found.

Rategan goes to the Fort. A guide shows him the courtyard wall where they were lined up. Rategan liked to examine places like this intensely, then close his eyes and see them being executed, their bodies …. what??
The walls are high, the drop to the sea deadly. Or they could have been burned. Or trucked off to the jungle. Wouldn't take much detective work to find out. But no-one does it. They want to erase Bishop and his comrades from the national memory. Same old.

He wonders whether there are any members of the New Jewel Movement out of jail, or alive.
Ricky the Rasta has the answer, proving once again the value of the connected taxi driver. He knows one of Bishop's closest cabinet ministers. The population of the Island is about 90-thousand. Everybody knows.
He makes a call or two and finds Sam Ramsamy, who is under house arrest.
After a brief phone conversation, he agrees to see Rategan.

Ramsamy is restricted to his family's bungalow on the Atlantic side. He is a thin man, thick mane of black hair, about 32, glasses, clearly traumatized. While the bodies of his friends and former cabinet colleagues lie somewhere unknown, he gets a pass. Why? Rategan never finds out.

He's been detained for 48 hours, interrogated by State department officials who'd been flown in and set up shop at a luxury yacht club.
"They were probably CIA," Ramsamy says.
Ramsamy's father is the biggest trader on the island and owns a grocery chain. He has studied at Concordia University in Montreal, and has a Ph.D in Marxism from the London School of Economics.

"This entire invasion was unnecessary. We went to Washington after the UN but Reagan snubbed us. We got a meeting with William Clark, his National Security advisor. We were open about everything: everything was on the table to prevent giving them a reason to invade. We guaranteed the safety of the Americans on the Island. We were even prepared to send the Cubans home, and let the Americans finish the airport. It wasn't for military purposes. It was to boost tourism. At one point Pat Buchanan[11] showed up and spewed anti-Communist rage at us. It was humiliating, very provocative. After we left, Maurice said an invasion was inevitable. I couldn't believe it, tried to reassure him. They were set on this course regardless of any offer we were making."

---

[11] Patrick Buchanan was Reagan's Communications aide and a right wing zealot.

Rategan has the phone number of the Governor-General. Sir Paul Scoon is a childhood friend of a Grenadian Doctor he plays cricket with in Toronto.

He calls and when he hears the name of his old friend, agrees to an interview.

"It will have to be at Government House. I'm confined to it."

Government House; another relic of Colonial Times looking as sad as an old dog who's lost his Master. Scoon, a courtly old man, tells Rategan he pretty well did what he was told.

The night before the invasion, with aircraft carriers and seven-thousand US troops poised offshore, a unit of Navy Seal Divers crash in through his front window, shaking the seawater out of their diving suits. Their commander walks up to Scoon, flips open a waterproof case, and has him sign a formal request for foreign military intervention.

"What could I do? Things had gone off the road here." He points to a large sash window above the portico.

"They came in there."

On his way out Rategan notices discarded ration packets dumped on the roof of the portico.

Out at sea, a handful of US and Royal Navy vessels loll in the sun.

Rategan is thinking about the script that's been followed here, redolent of invasions everywhere.

Whip up popular support by any means possible: The American students, the Cuban airfield.
Cross the T's and dot the I's: the divers and the Governor-General.
Cut the head off the snake (Bishop) and Promise a New Dawn. The executions and then, the mantra: "God Bless Reagan. God Bless Thatcher."

Time to leave. He has a heck of a documentary in his bag. With all the other foreign journos back in Barbados, he has had the place to himself, dodging anyone who might enforce Reagan's news blackout from the island itself. Official news of the deaths at the mental hospital, for example, was delayed as long as possible. But it was headed for Canadian radio in a matter of hours.

As Rategan prepares to leave, the 9-year old boy, named Fortune, Mrs. Brown's grandson, dogs his every move, asking questions.

"Where is Canada? Is it beautiful like here?"

He has a hunch, presses record, pulls out his mike.

"What's your name?"
"Fortune."

"How old are you?"

"Nine."

"What's your favourite subject?"

"Math."

"What's one and one?"

"Two."

"Two and Two?"

"Four."

"Four and four."

"Eight."

His sweet face smiling, feeling it.

"Eight and Eight?"

"Sixteen."

"Sixteen and Sixteen?"

He thinks. Mrs Brown giggles

"Tirty-four."

"Fortune."

"Ya?"

"What happened to Maurice Bishop?"

"Dem tek him up to the Fort, and dem kill 'im."

"Why?"

"I don't know why..."

They call Grenada Spice Island. Blossoms abound all over. Frangipani, hibiscus, ginger lily. On the way to the airport to catch the next flight out, he passes a perfume store.

The perfume is in glass containers, with cork stops and hand-written titles.

"Mystery Dancer."

"Midnight Lover."

He finds one with a musky aroma and the perfect name.
"Jump Up And Kiss Me".
He gets it for his fiancee.

There is also a glass case of island gems on little black
stone stands.
Opals, milkstone and quartzes. One handsome quartz
on a chain catches Rategan's eye. The price tag has the
words "New Jewel Pink" on it.
The sales lady turns it in the light.
"If you turn it in the sun, you'll see it has a pinkish
colour."
There it is.

Ricky the Rasta brings Fortune to see him off. He gives
Ricky the rest of his US dollars.
"Here." he says to Fortune.
He hands him the quartz.
Fortune is bug-eyed, turning it in his palm.
"You know what it's called?"
"No?"
"Read the tag stuck on the back."
"New Jewel Pink."
Fortune's mouth forms an O of conspiracy.
He clutches the stone and looks up at Rategan.
"Tank-you Rategan."
He nods.
"Remember. OK?"
"You come back some day Rategan?"
"When you are Prime Minister."

As the small UN plane he catches circles out towards
Barbados, he can still see Fortune waving.
And the madman singing.

"Home Home on the range
Where the deer and the antelope play.
Where seldom is heard a discouraging word
And the skies are not cloudy all day"

4 RATEGAN DOES PERU

Once again, Rategan has been dumped by a beautiful woman in Toronto and wants, or at least some part of him wants, to get shot covering the most dangerous story he can find. Just totally perforated against a wall in some tropical country.

He reads a story about the Sendero Luminoso (Shining Path) in Peru - radical guerrilla terrorists who control the source of eighty-five percent of the world's cocaine. He plonks the story down in front of David Studer, the guy who runs documentaries at *The Journal*.

"This would make a great doc."

A few days later he flies out of Toronto on a plane to Lima with a Newfoundland soundman, his Quebec shooter and a correspondent who has been stuck in newsrooms for years. Rategan has heard that a Swedish documentary crew were the only ones to get in with Sendero Luminoso and they had been executed and tossed into the Huallaga River, seen bobbing downstream. He can't wait.

He had contacted an old friend, Bob Carty, who is encyclopedic about Latin American resistance movements. Bob tells him Sendero is a unique and fascinating combination of Maoism and Indianismo led by a disciplined academic, a Doctor Guzman.

Bob delivers a contact, in Toronto - a Peruvian man and a Canadian woman who had gone to Peru for her master's thesis and joined the Revolution. They work out of half a tiny office off Yonge Street beneath a gay dance club.

Rategan introduces himself, explains his job at the CBC and that they don't pay and then provides credentials and contact information.

Then:

"My program is interested in finding out how Sendero Luminoso fits into the cocaine business. I want to go to Peru and go to the coca fields and get in with Sendero. I'd appreciate a briefing about Sendero and the situation of the conflict with the government, and, if possible, arrangements made for me and my crew to travel into coca territory held by Sendero and get the position on the ground."

This is the first step: you have to get access.

They ask a bunch of questions. It's a bit like an ideological job interview. The Peruvian man says little, but observes with berry-bright eyes. His face and body have the millennial hardness of the centuries-abused aboriginal.

You can see the moment when they trust you, when the green light flicks on in their eyes. When they see there's enough in it for them, their cause. And never, ever ever betray that. You have met with people that intelligence agencies would love to know and death squads would love to execute.

The woman asks him when he will be there, in Peru, and where will he stay.

A few days later he gets a call to meet at the same place. Only the woman is there. She asks him to listen carefully.

On the Monday after his arrival, at 2.30 pm in the afternoon, he is to exit his hotel in Miraflores; turn right and right again, go for four blocks, walk along that street until, on the left, he sees a sign for a dance studio. He will see a woman in a red scarf, cutting a hedge. Follow her inside. When he starts scribbling this down she says with a cold snap,

"Don't write anything down. Can't you remember it? Repeat it back to me."

He does.

"One question," he asks.

"Yes?" Impatient.

"You're Canadian, right?"

"Uh-uh."

"Why are *you* doing this?"

"Why am *I* doing this?" She pauses. "Massacre." The Spanish pronunciation. MASSAK-RA.

"What massakra?" he asks. But she pushes her hand out to him, her right finger wagging no.

"Be careful." And. "Promise me."

"What?"

"On that Monday. If you are being followed. Don't go."

"Of course."

"If she is not there, clipping the hedge, keep moving and do not go back."

ONE WEEK LATER. LIMA. PERU.

Foreign Documentary directors depend on fixers. Fixers are local people who meet you at customs with all the papers and with a vehicle that can transport you, the crew and the gear to the right hotel, and supply a porter to lug the gear. They know where and from whom to get the story, how to keep from getting arrested, kidnapped or killed, and when things go ker-blooey, as they will in Peru, where to get the best, or nearest, Pisco Sours. And after you've gone, they're left to clean up your mess. All for 100 dollars a day.

Because they don't get to leave, and the documentary you air hurls shit at their government, they might get killed. You will take care of their families. That was *The Journal* way.

Rategan has two fixers on this shoot. Carlos, a Peruvian desperate to make his own docs, who is great, and Chas Knight, an American radio freelancer who had been a Jesuit seminarian in California. His Spanish is perfect and he talks like he knows everyone. Knight has been to the town of Tingo Maria in Cocaine Valley twice and that's where Rategan wants to go. They are waiting for official authorization to travel there which will take three days for every one day you are told it will take, so, for now, he's stuck in a nightmare of a Lima traffic jam, chain-smoking, rolling his eyes and jonesing for Pisco Sours.

The scheduled Tuesday flight to Tingo Maria has no room for them. They book on the Thursday flight.

One way of killing time profitably is to find people in the city whose job it is to know what's going on. The *political* attachés at the various embassies. Chas Knight, the fixer, knows that the DEA boss for all of

Latin America, Aldo Marchicciano, is in Lima at the US Embassy and sets up meetings with him and the political attaché at the Canadian embassy.

On the second floor of the fortress that is the American Embassy, they can hear Marchicciano laughing uproariously as they walk along the carpeted corridor to his office. He waves them in while bellowing down the phone.

"It'll fucking kill him. Give him a kick in the ass from me... Yeah... yeah... copy me on that... (laughter)... ok... ciao yeah ciao baby."

Phone slams down, making everyone jump.

"Station Chief in Colombia getting his retirement party. So... The Canucks! Canuckstan." Shoving a big arm out.

He is a rough-faced movie mobster with a handgun in his belt. He is incredulous, amused that they are heading up to such dangerous territory, but is happy to confirm that the situation in the Upper Huallaga valley is a drug "war".

"If anyone guarantees your security, they are lying."

He tells them if they bump into any Americans up there, they don't officially exist. His "dudes" are there at the request of the oligarchs, the rich families that have plantations up there, sort of "freelance, independent consultants '*if you know what I mean*.' Not for public consumption."

"This is off the record, right?" he declares three times.

"Off, off, off Broadway, baby," he adds.

"You'll have a helluva film if you figure out a way to get inside Sendero and come out alive. HELLUVA FILM! OLIVER STONE. OLIVER FUCKING STONE" he bellows. "GOOD LUCK," suggestively raising his eyebrows at the comely correspondent, "I wish *I* was coming,"

The Canadian attaché is as unwelcoming as the DEA was welcoming. A Mr. Moore from Brandon, Manitoba advises Rategan in the strongest possible terms *not* to go *anywhere* near Tingo Maria. That if they do go to said Tingo Maria or anyplace in the Upper Huallaga Valley they are completely on their own *against* the *explicit* advice of the Canadian government. In fact, if they do go then this meeting they are now having has not taken place.

"This is an organization which has clearly expressed a level of repeated and lethal hostility towards people who do what you do."

He is clearly convinced they will all be killed and he doesn't relish the job of mailing brown paper envelopes to the families.

They have to kill time in the capital but they aren't allowed to take any TV shots in downtown Lima because of "seguridad". There are three ruthless guerilla organizations who have sworn to kill any government official they find.

They can shoot outide Lima, in the poor areas. They go to the zonas pobres, hillsides covered with slums with hundreds of thousands living in homemade shacks, no running water, kids in rags with skin rashes, feral cats, skinny dogs and plump rats, line-ups for water, one tap per 10-thousand people, sewerage running in open gullies, the daily trek up the mountainside foraging for firewood, young men in frayed Yankees t-shirts running past, their eyes sizzling with rage. Perfect conditions for a Revolution.

Eventually somebody shows up and denies them permission to shoot because they haven't been approved by "the committee". For this they must pay…in US dollars.

Fuck that. Rategan never pays. Almost.*

On the way back to town, Carlos hears on a military channel on his walkie-talkie about emergency food distribution in a barrio up the hillside that is getting out of hand. Lines started forming at 1 o'clock for flatbed trucks that don't get there until 3, because of an argument about paying the armed guards and soldiers without whom the sacks of grain will not be passed out. Then, at the last minute, the truck drivers want more money from government officials, and then the truck owner wants a bigger cut. The jammed little gears of corruption. By the time one truck backs up towards the queue, ravenous people who have been waiting in the heat for three hours are seething, ready to explode.

Rategan knows it's one of those moments he should call the crew off, withdraw, but he risks staying.

Then there is a new argument with thuggish looking hustlers who push their way in front of the mothers and children who'd been waiting in the severe heat and dust with their little pink slips. The crew is on the flatbed with Luc, the heavily-bearded Quebecker, who is shooting off the tripod when the crowd blows up. It is every man, woman and child for him or herself, clawing at the grain bags, tearing at each other, screaming, then beaten back with whips, automatics firing skywards, more screaming. A woman, skinny and burned brown, claws Rategan's arm as she reaches for the back of the truck, her nails tearing into his skin. In Spanish, she screams...

COMIDA PARA MI HIJO
("FOOD FOR MY CHILD.")

He would carry a three-inch long scab on his forearm for weeks.

Luc bails, passing the seventy-thousand dollar camera down to him, and off they go, into the van and down the rutted hilly road to the safety of the middle-class area, Zona Rosa, and the four-star hotel where they are staying.

Rategan makes sure his crew are safe and sound in the screening suite and goes back out to buy some scotch and a case of beer for them.

Still covered in dust from the riot, with blood from the fingernail scratch on his sleeve, he re-enters the hotel lobby. There, leaning against the flowered wallpaper outside the restaurant, is his favourite Canadian Prime Minister; the now-retired Pierre Trudeau.

Rategan walks up to him.

"Mr. Trudeau, Rategan Edwardes, CBC."

The doleful eye, the soft hand shake.

"You don't remember me but I ambushed you outside of Foreign Affairs a few years back...about cruise missiles."

"Ah yes."

Like all the great politicians he pretends to remember.

"Of course."

Trudeau gazes back towards the restaurant. He is waiting for someone.

"If I may ask, what are *you* doing here?" Rategan asks.

"I'm waiting for my sons," he nods towards the restaurant. "We just got in from the Galapagos. And you? What are you doing here?"

"I'm shooting a documentary, for the CBC"

"Oh. On what?"

"Maoist guerrillas who control the cocaine business."

Pause.

"Ahhh." Trudeau looks right at Rategan, appraising him, and with a glint in his eye says,

"*My kind of people.*"

"Hah... Indeed. That's good. Well. We're hoping to fly up there tomorrow." Then, from God knows where, Rategan says to Trudeau.

"You should come with us."

"Mmmmmm. I'll have to think about that," says Trudeau, appearing to actually consider it. *Leave the kids. Pop up for a few days to hang out with a bunch of murderous cocaine guerrillas.*

Rategan tries something else. After all, this is one of those famous people, like John Lennon, that Rategan's convinced, would enjoy him, if he could just get him alone for half an hour.

"We were just at a food riot."

Trudeau turns to him, slightly amused by the producer's persistence.

"The crew's a bit rattled and I'm just bringing them some refreshments. You're welcome to join us in the Ambassador Suite on the fifth floor if you like."

"Very tempting, thanks."

Pushed forward by a nanny, his tousled-haired sons emerge from the restaurant. Trudeau slips his hand onto their happy heads,

"I'm afraid the boys and I are off to dinner with our Ambassador."

"Too bad. Oh well. Next time."

"Indeed."

"Yes." Then, after a pause, he turns to Rategan with a serious tone.

"I'd be careful up there if I were you. I'm told those guys can be rather unfriendly."

Rategan nods appreciatively, knowing his chance is gone with The Great Canadian, but he will always remember the twinkle that passed between them.

"*My kind of people.*"

His friend, Bob Carty, in Toronto, has given him the name of a presidential contact, a woman in Lima.

"Give her a call. I've told her to expect you. She's a Quebecker who has studied Peru and has lived there for years. She has very interesting connections. She's in a very sensitive position, so tread lightly. She has to be careful. She will meet you but on what the New York Times calls deep, deep background. You must be discreet, and, under no circumstances, quote her. You cannot interview her on camera."

Rategan wants to meet this woman just to unpack the mystery of her. Sure enough, after he leaves a message, a handwritten note appears at his hotel on day two.

Meet me at Las Pequenas Lenguas (The Little Tongues) 11 pm tonight.

Meet who?

He assumes it must be Bob's Quebecoise.

On the way in a cab he notices soldiers on practically every corner, two or three of them, guns glinting under the streetlamps, clearly expecting a fight. He instinctually gets out two blocks from the address.

It's instinctual because he isn't working from a manual. He hasn't trained in spycraft, it's just common sense. Commonsense when you operate on the assumption that the people with the guns hate interfering gringos and would shoot you in a heartbeat.

The small brass fist in the door of Las Pequenas Linguas depicts a profusion of wormy tongues wriggling out of a clamshell. At the back of the dark, curved bar, all but concealed between some plants and a curtain of glass beads, is the Quebecoise.

Christiane's conversation is easy-going and ebullient. The bartender produces her drink like a magician and melts away. He brings Rategan a Pisco Sour. A good-looking, small man joins them.

"This is Juan. You didn't meet him."

Juan shakes Rategan's hand, and immediately commences his briefing in perfect Harvard English.

"You've come at a bad time. There's the possibility of a coup, and there's an election coming up with some very powerful candidates. Plus there are three low intensity guerrilla wars the military is involved in. People are turning up dead every day across Peru. Your story is an incredible one, but you will never, in four weeks, get to the truth of it, and come out alive. You may be able to get ... how would you say? ... marginal impressions by leaving the city because (and here he purses his mouth) poof.. things here in Lima could explode at any time and anything you have to do you have to get permission and nobody has the time or the interest in monitoring a Canadian TV crew doing that story."

He turns to Christiane and murmurs something, brushing her cheek with his lips. And then he is gone. Rategan blinks and turns to Christiane.

He senses they are lovers.

"He works in the President's office"

"In my experience people telling you to leave proves it's a Big Story".

"Maybe. But not advisable, all the same."

"The Co-" Rategan barely has the word cocaine formed, and her finger is on his mouth, shutting him down with an admonishing glance. Simultaneously Christiane gestures for another Pisco Sour from a bartender who seems like a well-oiled supporting actor in this slinky, shadowed performance.

She leans in and whispers in his ear. He gets a whiff of her perfume, eternal bliss here and gone in a nanosecond.

"So the official advice is to go back to Canada." He feels her sliding a paper into his jacket pocket, then, leaning back, audibly,

"Take the trip up to Cuzco, Macchu Picchu. It's safe. Up there the shamans still worship the leaf," and swivels off her chair. She stands before him, shrugging on her coat.

"If you do persist, and survive, do come and see me before you leave. I love to hear about the country. It is so rare I am able to get out of the city nowadays."

She touches his elbow, squeezes, and is gone, like a spirit in silk.

For a moment Rategan is not sure that anyone was there. He gestures into the dark and the bartender appears.

"La cuenta, por favor."

With a brief smile and the slightest raising of his hand the bartender makes it clear the drinks were paid for.

He waits until he is back in his hotel room. Every now and then, the tatata of automatic weapons and klaxons pierce the night.

He now does something he has done automatically ever since South Africa. He scrutinizes his room, assuming there are cameras in the ceiling, in the corners of the ceiling, in the TV set, in the bathroom. He pads outside to the balcony, kneels down, takes Christiane's piece of paper out, lights up a cigarette and reads.

"Padre Michel. Aucayacu."

He burns the paper then kicks the ashes through the ornate railings into the street below. The glowing scrap spirals down and dies as it hits the asphalt.

Merci Christiane.

Father Michel. Aucayacu.

On the Monday he gives the crew the day off.

At 2.30 that afternoon he heads out of the hotel, turning right. Two blocks up Friedrich Engels, he turns right again. Calle Diderot. On cue, fifty yards away, he sees her. A dark-haired woman in a long patterned black dress, white camisole, red scarf, clipping her hedge.

He approaches her and slows down. She looks at him, turns into the garden. He follows her, noting the wooden sign with "Studio de Danza" burned in with the shape of a dancer. Her fine, black hair is tied tight in a plaited ponytail that runs down between her two shoulder blades. He follows her, ducking through the open lower half of an old stable door into a cool space, immediately peaceful. There are wooden floors, white gossamer curtains over the windows, a long mirror and the barre on one side and two long benches on the other where Rategan imagines tired dancers sitting rubbing their feet, like a study by Degas. On the walls simple paintings of dancers in rich floral skirts in various arabesques. A kid's wall hanging, Pace et Amore, a tree of life, birds.

She gestures to a bench, and "Would you like some tea?" Spanish-accented American English.

"Por Favor. Con leche. No azucar." She smiles and goes through a doorway into a kitchenette. He hears her fiddling with cups, a kettle, a fridge door. She comes out with a small tray and two cups, a small jug of milk, a China bowl of sugar cubes with a doily covering.

"Is this your studio?"

"Yes. I teach Peruvian dance mostly, autentico. Folklorico."

They sip and put down their cups. It is so cool here, a world apart from the dusty anarchy of Lima's streets. One can barely hear a passing siren on a nearby street.

It's one of those moments Rategan experiences in foreign places in which he could stay forever. This woman and her cause. Way past time to take sides, he is thinking. "Everybody knows."

It falls very quiet except for a low buzzing sound above their heads.

"Your English is better than my Spanish. Apologies," he says.

"No problem."

"You are Rategan."

He nods like a hypnotist's sideman.

"Our Canadian friends have told us about your objective here."

"And you are?"

"You don't need a name. I'm sure you understand."

"Of course."

"My message is short, anyway."

Uh-oh, he thinks. No green light. But liquid brown eyes.

"These are the worst of times, so my news is not good. For you."

Rategan nods.

She holds herself like a racehorse forced to be still, all the running coiled in political concentration. The way the world works on his mind, in intrusive flashes, he knows that she will be killed or jailed before he dies.

"The position (pronouncing it *posiss-yon*) of our organization is" that Her cadence and delivery changes, the warmth now ice.

And now the official statement

One finger raised.

"One. We do not dialogue with the foreign media."

Two fingers.

"Two. Chairman Guzman does not give interviews to foreign media."

Third finger, the dull clink of her rings.

"Three. We direct you to the third edition of El Diario, of May 1988, where Chairman Guzman gives our position on the issue of the coca farmers."

She is done. There's nothing more. They stare at each other for a long beat, like the record got stuck.

"This is all I am authorized to say."

She's carried the message. Rategan knows when his pitch lies doomed. There's a buzzing sound, from above. In the ceiling.

Now, the soft leave. Make contact on some other plane, so that if they soften, you may get that access or that interview.

Rategan had taken dance lessons at the Toronto Dance Theatre and has seen Ailey, Sibley and Nureyev perform, so they spend the rest of the time talking about that. He thinks she tears up when he describes seeing Ailey and his company in Manhattan. After a while he says,

"Well, I shall leave you. Respect to you and your people. But regardless of your advice, I'm going to Upper Huallaga anyway. I leave you with this. Someone like me is the best way for your organization to get your message out to the English–speaking world. You can trust me. Please tell your people that I'll be there next week with a camera crew and I'll be asking about the coca business and America's involvement in the drug war."

He has stood up. She is looking at him slightly bemused, but not without sympathy. The Dancer's Grace. He again feels that unnerving rush of warmth that is inappropriate, counter-productive, and clumsy.

He looks firmly at her and says -

"And I'd like you to tell your comrades, if you don't mind. *NOT* to kill us. Okay?"

She raises her eyebrow for a moment, and then looks at him directly. Steely.

"Okay" she says. "But I would not have completed my task if I didn't stress to you that our organization will *not* be assisting you in any way. At all."

Rategan offers his hand, which is smoothly taken. A cold, fine, strong grip. She is the sister, the lover, of dead men.[12]

"Don't worry." he says. "I can let myself out. You don't have to come outside. Gracias."

"De nada," she whispers.

---

[12] *1992. The National Directorate Against Terrorism (DIRCOTE) began surveying several residences in Lima because agents suspected that terrorists were using them as safehouses. One of them was operating as a dance studio supposedly inhabited by only one person, the dance teacher. The DIRCOTE operatives routinely searched the garbage taken out from the house and it was noticed that the household produced more garbage than one person could account for. Furthermore, agents found discarded tubes of cream for the treatment of psoriasis, an ailment that Guzmán was known to have. On September 12, 1992, an elite unit of the DIRCOTE raided the residence. On the second floor of the house, they found and arrested Guzmán and eight others. All the while Rategan was with the dance teacher, his big scoop, Guzman, may have been upstairs, a few feet away, through the buzzing ceiling. And he'd missed it.*

It takes Rategan the full walk back to the hotel to shake off the effect she has had on him and focus on what has to be done next.

Rategan has heard that the Peruvian government has an official, but secret, warehouse in Lima filled with the purest cocaine on the planet, 98 percent pure, designated for a few big players in the pharmaceutical industry. And Coca Cola, its rumoured.

Carlos the fixer knows somebody who knows someone related to the manager of the secret warehouse and if Rategan visits with a one hundred dollar bill placed in his passport, then maybe …

So, at six pm, after hours, Rategan finds himself in an industrial area in front of big white metal gates with padlocks and chains. A slot opens up and eyes appear, look, and slam the slot shut again. The iron gate's barrel bolt scrapes along its rusted track as it opens and the van with Carlos and Luc is waved hurriedly into an open courtyard. A loud metal slam behind them. Out of the lone tree in the middle of the yard vultures rise and settle back, screeching and flapping.

Long, low sleek sheds surround them. Three furious German shepherds bark from an enclosure, then fall silent as Rategan is directed into an office overlooking the yard. A handsome, perky man with an open–necked shirt gestures him into an inner office.

They exchange the ritual courtesies of the Spanish meeting.

"Buenos Noches, Señor."

"Buenos Noches."

Rategan explains the documentary and slides his passport across to the man.

*The man's eyes slide over the exposed greenback.

"Dies minutos, Senor, no mas."

He barks an order, and waves them out. Rategan gestures to Luc waiting inside the van. After various unlockings they are led into one of the sheds.

"We have ten minutes, Luc."

Beauty shots of cocaine.

In wooden bins, on one side and metallic containers on the other, lies pure, pungent, glistening snow-white cocaine. The manager takes a large scoop and plunges it into a bin, turning the cocaine like the finest white flour. The air in the shed shimmers.

The aisle between the rows of cocaine is very narrow, so Luc has to lean against one bin to shoot the ones opposite. Rategan sees that stuck across the back of his dark blue windbreaker is now a thumb-wide line of 98 percent pure, government-owned Peruvian cocaine. Rategan figures about 2-thousand dollars worth on a Canadian street.

Rategan is no stranger to the tug of cocaine; but never on the job. He's learned that up in the Andes the fresh coca leaves are placed in a tin bath with water, lye and an acid. Then, Indian campesino boys as young as eight years old, tread on this mix for 36 hours straight. The acid eats into their bare feet. The solution becomes a paste, *pasta basica*, like a lump of gasoline mud, which is then packed and flown for further refinement to Colombia and then cut again, packaged and flown to the US and Europe.

Through Carlos, he arranges to pay a few addicts to smoke *pasta basica* on camera. *Pasta Basica* is cheap and accessible and a big addiction problem in Peru. Rategan's not sure he'll use it in the final doc but with the weather and permit delays, they might as well keep busy. Also he doesn't know how much of the story he's going to get in the mountains.

The leader of the trio of addicts is a post-graduate university student who's having trouble finding a job, and two street friends of his, hustlers in the currency market. They're happy to get a big chunk of free pasta because they don't seem to care about much else.

They meet in an oily, disused garage in an alley at the edge of the city. They thumb a wedge of the paste into a broken bottleneck and fire up. The smell is overwhelming, toxic, acidic. It must be tearing holes in their lungs. The student inhales, his eyelids slide ecstatically, his head kicks back softly, as the coke smoke hits his upper chest. He slumps back into an old couch, his chin falling forward onto his chest. The effect is immediate and catatonic. The other two do likewise, passing the bottleneck like a demonic chalice. Luc shoots and all Rategan can hear is the soft whirring of the betacam. Luc glances sideways at Rategan.

Rategan gives him the thumb-across-the-throat "cut" sign. They have their sequence. They leave the three men sprawled. As they pack up the gear the men stir and grunt, satisfied. The student's eye opens, and he gives a thumbs up to Rategan. Rategan leans in, as if to a doomed angel, and slips him another hundred dollar bill.

"Gracias, hombre. Sweet dreams."

And they are gone, silent, as Carlos drives the van carefully out of the dark alley and onto the lit streets.

"*Merde,*" murmurs Luc.

"*Muerto antes de Navidad,*" says Carlos.

Dead by Christmas.

⟝——◆——⟞

Finally the permit comes through, the weather clears, and they fly over the Pacific coastline and up into the mountains. It's a view tourists would pay thousands for.

They have made it to Tingo Maria. A whorehouse town at the edge of the jungle and the drug war.

They are billeted in a Government Tourist Lodge on the outskirts with only bug-mesh and wood slats to separate them from the deep, dark jungle. A jungle inhabited by the loudest nocturnal creatures Rategan has ever heard. Birds screech and cackle pretty well all day long. And toads and bats and owls and insects create a cacophony all night long.

Staying at the same 'lodge' are "The Butterfly Collectors," a cover for a dozen ex-Vietnam special forces dressed in jungle civvies, wrapped in weaponry. They are seconded to the Drug Enforcement Agency. Sendero Luminoso is competing with three oligarch families in the valley for control of the coca fields. And the DEA gunmen are there to make sure the controllers of the coca crop are Uncle Sam's motherfuckers not Mao's motherfuckers.

The first morning Rategan asks the Americans,

"What are you guys doin' here?"

"Who wants to know?"

"Canadian documentary producer here."

"Uh. Uh. Weeell, we're butterfly collectors."

They're sticking to that cover. All night these guys drink and fuck prodigiously then fly off in the pre-dawn in their choppers, armed to the teeth. Rategan wants to crack 'em open, to go out with Luc and shoot some action; but they aren't yielding. Underneath the wild cowboy behaviour is military discipline.

So one night Rategan announces to a few of them,

"If I can drink you guys under the table, you have to tell me what is really happening here."

They take up the challenge. They are sprawled around a big table beneath a stuffed wild deer, a bug-eyed wild pig, a twenty foot long anaconda skin and a long-dead fox baring its stained teeth. Peruvian pipe and guitar music plays softly on a suspended speaker.

They are sticking to the butterfly hunting story. It's a good cover. Moths as big as hands bat themselves into the wire mesh, bats as big as flying rats.

When they exchange names they are clearly fictitious, so Rategan makes up his own. On his right sits Silverado, a silver-haired dude with a silver revolver in a black leather holder studded with silver stars. On his left is The Silent One, who looks a bit like Peter Fonda in Easy Rider and never takes his shades off. Sitting opposite is a feral southerner with bad teeth, crouched and fidgeting with his Southern Comfort. He introduces himself.

"M'name's Ratfucker. Ah'm frim Joe-ja."

It's now about three in the morning. All four of them are now pretty hammered on multiple Jack Daniels, but Rategan privately, feels in control.

The Silent One suddenly sits erect and expressionless. Rategan thinks he is going over and over something in his past that went terribly wrong. Christopher Walken in Deer Hunter chest-high in water in the Viet Cong holding pen.

The Silent One stands up and leaves. He's got long bowed legs. Rategan figures it's from riding horses in Texas or playing hockey in Minnesota.

Ratfucker announces-

"Two hours to fuck. And two hours of sleep. What's a man to do?" and he leaves too.

Silverado stares at his glass, then looks into Rategan's eyes for a while. He finally leans forward with the sincerity of a southern preacher.

"Ok. You seem like a straight-up guy. First of all, officially, we are not here. The DEA hooked us up. We're US Navy counter-insurgency. SEALs. Okay? The job here is to drive Sendero out of the coca business, and keep the old families, who are pro-US, in charge. And you never heard that from me, 'cos they're not saying that in Washington."

He waves the bartender to bed.

"Sendero. You know about them. Look out. Vicious little fuckers. As badass a bunch as I've ever come across. They went into a village up the valley a couple of weeks back, took all the kids out of the local school, lined up their teachers, gave a lecture on the inadvisability of co-operating with the government and then executed the teachers. Shot them in front of the kids."

Sips. Stares at a thudding sound in the night.

"We're teaching the local military how to fight back, push Shining Path back off the coca fields. That's all I can tell you. It's an 18 month contract."

"Is it working?"

An animal screams nearby, the sound of rustled bush.

"Nothing works with coke. The demand is relentless, the money is huge. It's grown in places you can't find. If you find 'em you can't reach 'em, unless to spray 'em.

The Columbians and some American freelancers fly it out every day, the Colombians process it and it gets through to the 20 million users in the States. 24/7."

Rategan senses this guy is in charge here, and probably has a degree.

"These peasants here grow it because it feeds their families. Other crops don't make subsistence income for them. We're just pushing back, giving them a bit of heat, reminding them who's boss. If it comes to that."

"The local anti-narcs. Any good?"

"They have some good people, but, hey. You've been around. It's Latin America. As soon as we leave, the bad guys move back in with the big bribes, the cars and the TVs. Whatcha gonna do?"

"Seen much action?" He put his hands out as if to say *enough.*

"Listen. I heard from Lima about you guys coming up. You're planning to go up valley, yeah?"

"Uh-uh."

"Don't. A Swedish TV crew went up there two months back. They'd been working on getting access to the Shining Path for years. Nice guy called Sven. About your age. Working with Peruvian expatriates in Scandinavia. Thought they were covered. Interview with Guzman, the whole deal. Got up to Aucayacu, were told to fuck off. But they crossed the river anyway, into Sendero territory. Bad move. They were taken prisoner by a bad little fucker called Commandante Fermin. And executed."

The jungle has fallen quiet. A chill, finally, at five in the morning. Silverado stands up, stretches his lanky body. He looks down at Rategan, who feels like shit, but who has got what he needs, if not the on-camera interview he wants.

"So that's the deal. We never had this conversation, ok?"

"Just a chat about butterflies."

"We're heading out tomorrow."

"Okay."

"Don't try and take any pictures of us, ok?" He turns to go.

At his back Rategan asks,

"What time are you leaving"

"Fuck you," tossed over his shoulder.

As he walks across the thick wooden floor his hand flicks out a little wave.

Rategan knows the shot he has to get.

As dawn outlines the massive trees outside the mesh, just as he heads for his bed, a bell shatters the peace. It's the amplification of the lodge's telephone. The night manager, roused from his sleep, waves Rategan over. His editors in Toronto have been trying to make contact through the broken phone system, but Rategan has so far managed to avoid having to talk to them.

He gives the manager the thumbs down, and turns to his room, collapsing into his own bed. He's drifting off when the banging starts. Ratfucker is on the job with a hooker who is whelping. He picks up the tempo. Rategan watches the wall next to his throbbing head bulge.

Another sleepless night in Paradise. Then -

Fuck, they killed the Swedes.

One More Thing. He rolls out onto his shaky feet. He stumbles into Luc's's cabin.

"Get up. Shoot the mercenaries leaving in the choppers. Please."

"Ok.. fuck.. Merde.. you stink.."

"I know. Sorry." and his falling body spins away, back down the corridor to thwack into his cot as the final wall-shaking wails burst from the adjacent hooker.

Two days earlier Rategan had sent his fixers, Carlos and Chas Knight, into town to ask people how safe things are up-valley. where they can contact coca farmers, Sendero units, and anything about Christiane's Canadian padre in Aucayacu. Carlos has come back to say that Chas is staying over with a priest friend, "To get further intel". Rategan smells a rat.

There's a call. Something has gone wrong. It turns out Chas's priest runs a small home for orphans in Tingo Maria and that Chas had picked up a boy. The boy had lured him to the river where an older brother and his friends are waiting and where they steal the money Rategan had given Chas, and had beaten him up. He was being held at the local police station.

Rategan hands Carlos Chas's per diem for the rest of the shoot and Carlos handles it beautifully. The police agree to a deal that Knight will report to Peruvian immigration if Rategan flies him back to Lima.

When they pick him up, Chas's face is bloated, shiny, and blotched with red welts, like he's been kicked a few times, but more dangerously, he is clearly coming down from something, several floors at a time.

"Listen man, I found out shit. Heavy shit. I can't tell you too much. They're listening. It's really heavy. You gotta call off the shoot. The Black Marias are onto you. Go back to Lima. This place is super dangerous. You can't stay. They're watching you, man."

He's like an overweight, strung-out Dennis Hopper.

His eyes dart. He is surging and ebbing.

"What are you on, man?"

"Huh?"

"What are you on?"

It turns out he has been taking a lot of cheap and powerful prescription drugs you can get hooked on from the pharmacies of a place like Peru. Drugs for sleep, drugs to stay awake, drugs not to drink, a whole cornucopia. Thus the shine, the rapid speech, the torrent of names.

He does have one priceless piece of information though. He confirms there's one foreigner left up valley in Sendero territory. And it is a Canadian priest they call Padre Michel.

Christiane's contact confirmed again.

"OK. But you, Knight. You gotta go," says Rategan.

Knight starts pleading.

"I can't go back to the States. Please don't tell Reuters, whatever you do."

Carlos and Rategan drive him to the airport. He grabs Rategan's arm.

"Don't go up there, man, this place is worse than the Wild West."

Rategan disengages.

"Listen to me. Stop taking the drugs. Find your way back to your God."

"Yeah. I will. I Promise. Thanks man. God bless. God ble..."

As they drive away, Rategan thinks the Catholic Church spawns some really bent people. And forgives them. Again. And again.

A few weeks later, he sees Chas Knight's byline on a Catholic newsite on two of Rategan's stories, pasta basica and the government cocaine sheds.

A story thief, to boot.

The Knight episode has unnerved his crew, especially his rant on how the trip will get them all killed. Rategan wants to go into the heart of darkness and they don't. The bad guys are winning in South Africa. He just got his heart shredded by a woman. To the heart of darkness seemed to him the place to head, a place of reality and seriousness where real beauty and real truth might reveal itself. Living anywhere safe felt like a form of cowardice.

The Huallaga River, the width of a football field churns between them and Aucayacu, where the Canadian priest lives. Until the rain stops, Carlos says the river is impassable. Brown waves cresting to four feet in the strong current.

The crew kills more time, playing cards, sleeping. On the satfone, The Desk gets through and the nervous foreign editor says perhaps Rategan, given the dangers and the weather, perhaps "we" should think about withdrawing to Lima.

"You can interview experts and we can use stock footage and stitch something together."

Rategan pretends to lose the line...

The rain finally stops. Perilously, on ropes and a big log raft, rocking and yawing across the swells, they get the van across the Huallaga.

The crew sullenly follows him into the van for the trip north. They came to a fork in the road. The one to the right leads 80 kilometers to Aucayacu and the war zone. The one to the left heads over the mountains and down to the coast.

In the middle of the road north is what looks like a bomb crater. It has pleated wire strung across it. Hanging from the wire is the skull of a small unrecognizable animal grinning maniacally and scratched into a piece of wood the words...

EL PODER NACE DEL FUSIL

Power is born in the barrel of a gun (Mao Tse Tung) and the letters TV with the No symbol slashed over it.

Daylight is fading.

"Let's move it. The Holiday Inn books up pretty fast." Rategan jumps out and walks backwards in front of the van, signaling it around the crater.

Silence envelops the road as they splash through puddles and potholes for the last half hour into Aucayacu, where there seems to be nothing much happening other than two kids on 125 cc Kawasakis blaring past them doing fishtails. The biker boys u-turn 100 yards away and blare by them again. Rategan shouts at the driver.

"Alto." The fact they have bikes makes them notable. Rategan has them pegged for scouts or couriers. He guesses they have been sent out to follow them. Gringoes. "Extranjeros." He assumes whoever controls these two little dudes knows who he is, why he's there, what he's looking for. If the Dance Teacher let them know.

"Que tal?" He makes a cutting gesture. They kill the bikes.

"Nosotros buscamos Padre Michel."

"Padre Michel?"

"Si. El Padre Canadiense."

They confer briefly.

"Yo es?"

"Television Canadiense."

More conferring.

"Momentito, Senor"

The younger one is sent off leaving blue farts of blattering smoke coming out of his bike. Rategan regards the boy that stays behind. He has a red bandanna round his neck. Bony chest with a nick scar on his breastbone, a frayed plaid shirt, red and yellow, open to his ribs. A machete in his belt. Maybe 14. A crow screams somewhere.

"Porque yo es nunca en escuela." Rategan asks.

"No hay escuela aqui."

"Porque?" The kid doesn't answer, and his expression suggests he doesn't miss school one bit.

The other kid returns, confers with the older boy who waves them to follow, and thence they arrive at the bungalow of Padre Michel Leblanc of the Oblate Missionaries of Holy Peace in Aucayacu, the last Missionary left up in the Upper Huallaga Valley and a character right out of Graham Greene.

"TV... Oooh... this is trouble," he says when he sees them, in a Franco-Ontarian accent, his hands on his cheeks. "But you are most welcome. Five of you. Mon Dieu. Four of you will have to share. Mademoiselle shall have her own chambre."

They are knackered. The long delay at the lodge, the trip up from Tingo, the river crossing, the journey into an unknown, hostile place has ground away at each of them. And they have very little usable footage to show for it. And an impatient desk back in Toronto.

Rategan gives the driver and Carlos money to go buy dinner and breakfast from wherever they can find it. Then he has a bath. And crashes. He has gotten everyone here.

Now the task is to a) get the story-in-pictures and b) not get anyone killed.

Father Michel turns out to be a Godsend. The only white man in Hell, a Canadian from Ottawa, one of theirs. So he assumes. He tells them right away they are the only non-Peruvians in town, and because it is a Sendero controlled community, no one will talk to them or help with the story. Every other foreigner but Michel has left. As far as this priest is concerned, the Peruvian government is racist towards the Indian population, has allowed agricultural prices to drop catastrophically, and has allowed education and health services to shrivel up and die.

"Sendero is much more representative of local communities. They attack poverty and despair, encourage self-reliance and self-esteem, offer a path out. A Shining Path. That the Church is struggling to match. The difference is, they promise salvation in *this* life."

He sounds like a booster for the Shining Path.

"But what about these stories of cruelty and the massacre of innocents?"

"Believe me." says the priest "the military and the police do the massacring around here. They bribe desperate people for information, and yes, Sendero executes informers."

"And you think they're justified."

"No. But, around here, things have become desperate. Growing Coca is the only way to make a living now. The practice of decades has recently turned deadly. So Sendero has organized self-defence for the coca farmers. Most of the Coca collectives around here are led by Sendero committees. The ordinary peasants are beautiful people caught between two devils. I have a small but very strong congregation, about 60 souls. They are the most committed, wonderful people I've ever known. But they are terrified. And you guys being here. To them, you are Martians arriving from another galaxy. To Sendero, a hostile Galaxy. And it's taken me 14 years to build trust. Please don't do anything to destroy that. OK?"

Later, in confidence, Father Michel tells Rategan he has spoken to a local Sendero Commander who will meet with him alone with his committee the next evening, but Rategan cannot tell anyone about this.

"They are very paranoid about military and police informers, and they absolutely believe that the colour of your skin defines you as possible CIA."

The first morning they go to the market. Luc knocks off some beauty shots. Indian women in bright red, gold and black dresses and display tables piled with potatoes, squashes, peppers, fruit, corn, kitchenware, cheap clothing.

A siren wails, and two military trucks speed up, disgorging armed men bristling with weaponry, their faces masked with black balaclavas.

One group secures the perimeter, shooing peasants out of the way. A second group escorts two soldiers carrying orange sacks.

They swarm the potato tables and fill the sacks. Same with the oranges and cassava.

An officer dumps a fistful of cash on an Old Woman, and they leave, the perimeter guard backing up with them, guns pointed at the sellers and buyers, until their buy is safely stashed. And, sirens blaring, they disappear in the dust.

It says something about who controls the town that picking up potatoes is a full-on military exercise.

Luc gets it all on-camera.

The next three days Rategan lives as a series of scenes.

Three scenes. The hearing, the verdict and the long march.

Scene one involves walking past the open door of a concrete garage-sized structure alongside a mud alley. This is the hearing. The priest has sent him there, with

Carlos and Kawasaki boy, to a community meeting of Sendero, to make his case.

It is late evening and the light from the meeting hall falls out into the street, where babies, young kids, cats and dogs play and sniffle. Rategan walks past, and looking in, sees a small man in mid-speech looking out above the heads of about twenty villagers. He is waved in, expected. He waits. The leader finishes, the crowd shouts -

"Viva la revolucion. Viva Commandante Guzman."

A numbers of girls and kids and women scream the slogans, so it's high, ear-piercing, incantatory.

When his turn comes it is an exercise in polite democratic discourse. He introduces himself, thanks them, acknowledges their courtesy, always showing respect. Everyone knows their history. The Indians of Andean and Amazonian America have been treated like non-people for centuries. Less than fully human. Nobody has ever cared what they think, as long as they don't think. Beasts of Labour. He acknowledges the difficulties they face. Poverty, racism, exclusion. He acknowledges the brutality of Imperialism and Colonialism. Carlos softly translates. In the low electrical light, their attention grows, staring at him, the intensity palpable, their reaction unreadable.

He describes Canada as a different place, a more prosperous place, a safe and fair nation where workers have rights and farmers' free organizations with recourse to laws that protect their livelihoods. He loves doing this sort of thing for the country that took him in from apartheid South Africa, a place so twisted and violent. He speaks about free media, how Canadians are interested in far-off places and their stories. He talks about how some young Canadians inhale cocaine and how much damage it does. He talks about how they have a right to grow what they can to feed themselves on their own lands. Their attention is now absolute, and while the atmosphere warms, this crowd is still not for moving. In other similar situations pitching for access around the world, the people believe that they can have this: that something like the Canadian dream is accessible to them. And they let you in. But here, these folks have been torn from connection, severed by lethal oppression.

Nonetheless he concludes by explaining his project with the camera crew, how he wants to get the opinion of the local people and tell the truth about Coca. The truth, for them. Sitting behind him are three of them, community representatives, who, he has been advised, are Sendero commanders, though it is forbidden to say so. And then he is done. A youth leader, a young woman in khakis who is tiny and fervent thanks him.

"Viva la Revoluçion. Vive Commandante Guzman.", and everyone dissolves into the night, down an alley lit by a single spluttering lamp.

As they walk back to the priest's house, the moon reflects off rain puddles on the dirt track, shining. Sendero. Luminoso. He loves the sound of it. And the idea. A shining, moonlit path in the darkness, the only road to salvation.

Two evenings later the man who addressed the garage gathering, comes to the priest's house. He takes off his hat and comes into the front room, sits down on a threadbare couch in front of the window so he is mostly a silhouette, accepts tea, exchanges pleasantries with Padre Michel and then speaks in a voice so thin and soft it is hard to hear. The answer, translated by Carlos, is the following...

"The Organization thanks you for explaining your position to the committee. The Organization however does not dialogue with the foreign media. The Organization believes that the children of the imperialists who use drugs are not the responsibility of the farmers of the Huallaga. The Organization has decided that no pictures will be allowed and you must leave Aucayacu immediately."

The opportunity is disappearing. At these moments, Rategan knows this meeting is the last chance to get *something*. Something to shoot. Something to take down the valley, and get to Canada for broadcast.

"One more thing."

"Yes?" says Rategan.

The peasant leader looks directly at him for the first time and says...

"La noche tiene los milles ojos."

The night has a thousand eyes.

Rategan chills. Although he recognizes the Maoist quote, given the context, the rainy, jungle-fringed village, it's a threat. It exactly describes the look he saw in the eyes of the washer woman when they had driven in. Clocked.

Rategan looks into the eyes of the man. He will not quit. He doesn't give a shit. So life ends here. He does not believe the man will carry out the threat. He believes that the man has been ordered to deliver the threat by those who will carry it out.

When his task is done, however, the man agrees to stay for frijoles y café y pan. They, the padre, Carlos and him, are solicitous of each other, almost tenderly respectful. Joaquin is a small man with hard hands and strength, the gaze of ages spent in hardship and want. The sharpest of the thousand eyes. Rategan gives him 200 US dollars for the community, and said he will pay a coca farmer another 300 dollars cash, US, if they can shoot his coca field and interview him. The Sendero word will not be mentioned. It's crass, but he's desperate. The man appears to waver. He agrees to seek permission for them to travel to the coca fields, on one condition. They don't mention the words Sendero Luminoso, and they don't ask the farmer any questions about Sendero. Rategan agrees, they shake, and he is gone. Rategan has forced his foot back in the door.

Rategan watches him leave, walking down the rain-coated paving stones that form a path to the metal gate with the catch-lock and the hedge on either side. Like the mining towns back in South Africa. Welkom, Stilfontein. Rategan watches him go.

The man turns left and the top half of his small head and hat is visible above the hedge. The soft shutter on Rategan's cortex opens and closes, and he knows the bob-bob-bob of his hat and the hedge, is an image he'll retain forever.

What privation, what struggle, what disappointment, has marked Joaquin's trek through life? There is not a jot of fat on his face, no complexity in his eye, and the pure grip of ideology is upon him. He'd be a formidable adversary. Killing him, as Guevera had said, wouldn't kill the idea. And thousands of him, killable yes; but the idea, inextinguishable.

The fountain at the roundabout has no water coming out of it. A softly swirling mist envelopes it, propelled by a silence that slips down from the mountains across the valley and the river and back up the other side to the heavens. Again, the scream of scavenging birds.

Rategan shudders at how easily he can imagine the mindset of the colonial mass murderer. Most of his contemporaries had served in the South African Defence Force, or worse.

His sympathies at that moment are very much with the Joaquins of the World.

As he turns inside, Father Michel is standing on the porch, with that smile of the missionary out on a limb, that all-embracing beneficence. That spirit-moves-in-mysterious ways wonderment. He nods towards where Joaquin had been sitting seconds before.

"I think he has decided to help you."

"Is it the money?"

He's non-committal.

"It will feed a family for months. And buy medicine."

THE MARCH.

Word comes late that night via the Kawasaki kids. Joaquin has come through. Rategan doesn't care if it was the money or the talk. It is on. After ten days.

They leave at 5 am for the hills. The crew finally has something to shoot. Led by Joaquin, after a two-hour drive northeast, they stop in a bowl of sheer, thick mountain slopes that disappear upwards into thick cloud. Then, on foot, up, up, up along a slippery, muddy path into the sky. Three local campesinos carry the gear. At one point, after an hour, Rategan stops, absolutely beat. The man in front of him carrying an equipment case and a tripod comes back down. He reaches into a pocket and offers him three coca leaves, gesturing to his mouth. He pats a rock, sweeps an arm over the view of the mist covering the forest below. Rategan sits down, pops two of the Coca leaves in his mouth, chewing the bitter green. The correspondent, all 100 pounds of her, comes up the path and rests with her porter. She's smiling for the first time all shoot. She has spent most of the time with earphones clamped on, listening to Chopin.

"What are we going to say?" she asks.

"Coca fields like these dot the Andean valleys. For the man who works this patch, it's money for him and his family. For The US government he's the enemy. Every now and then plane flies over, spraying insecticide. But on the ground Sendero Luminoso is a friend of the coca farmer... something to that effect"

She has her spiral notebook out.

"Write it out in your own style," he says. "We'll fine-tune it once we get up there. You'll nail it."

"Okay. I'll need some time to fix my face."

It is red with exertion and her hair is straggled with sweat.

Once they get under way the coca juice kicks in, and Rategan feels a lightness of being. The muddy, slippery rocks seem shaped to his footfalls, and he is bouncing *upwards*. He falls into a trance, concentrating on the handmade multi-coloured belt of the Indian in front of him, and his ascent becomes, if not buoyant, mysteriously effortless. The coca has banished his fatigue and he understands. He understands that any consumption of this herb, corrupted by chemistry and the dollar *far* away from here, is too far from its God, and will have no good issue.

But this use of it is ancient and fortifying.

About an hour later they break through the jungle into a couple of acres of coca on a flat parcel of land snug between green peaks. The chances of any DEA plane finding this meadow, let alone dusting it with poison must be a trillion to one and there are hundreds of them in these breathtaking Andean foothills.

On cue, the sun comes out, bathing the acreage in brilliant lime green. Luc calmly takes his shots as the gold breaks in and out of scudding clouds.

He sets up for the on-camera.

She nails it first time.

Now the promo.

"On the Journal, the story of Peru's Cocaine Valley." "When we get back, into the heart of Cocaine Valley, (pause for an edit) on The Journal." "Next week, on the Journal, Cocaine Valley."

They interview the Sendero farmer. He is a simple man who talks like farmers everywhere about yields per acre, soil and weather and market fluctuations of coca versus millet, rice and beans; talks about the one time a plane had flown over; and talks about, yes, how the 'community'(code for "Sendero") protects his fields; he even parrots the quote about how the addictive consumption of cocaine by the children of the imperialists is not his responsibility.

"Is Sendero a help or a hindrance to you?"

Rategan has broken his promise to not to mention Sendero, and wonders if the Sendero commander will act, but the farmer answers the question without hesitation.

"Sendero is our salvation and our protector. For it, we will die."

They pause. Birdsong and a gentle wind. A cloud shadows his field.

Time to head back down. Rategan pops the third coca leaf and as they glide down, a soft rain begins to fall.

At the bottom, in the gathering dark, Luc gasps at Rategan. He has clouds of steam emanating from his body.

Rategan stands there, feeling exquisite, steaming like a volcano. Everyone is smiling, even the Sendero man.

They have the doc. They turn for home.

Pisco Sours await.[13]

---

[13] Carlito's recipe for Pisco Sours
- 2 ounces pisco brandy
- 1 ounce <u>simple syrup</u>
- 3/4 ounce key lime juice
- 1 large egg white
- 2 to 3 dashes aromatic bitters

5 RATEGAN DOES DUNDAS AND SHERBOURNE.

Within weeks of walking out of the CBC, Rategan is starting up as an independent documentary filmmaker.

He's in downtown Toronto, out in the soft summer rain, filming a hooker.

She pirouettes for each passing truck and car. She's all lit up in her finery, silver shimmering top, dyed blonde hair, black fishnet stockings, white leather mini. Like a cheap decoration that's broken out of a dollar store. She's standing at the corner of Dundas and Sherbourne, on the north-west side, just past the alley, where the old mansions are set back from the road. They're dark, brooding rooming houses. Rategan thinks they provide a nice gloomy backdrop for the hooker strutting her glittering stuff. He darts across the street to introduce himself.

"Hi."

"Hi cowboy."

"I'm making a film."

"I see that."

"Can I get a shot of you?"

"It's gonna cost ya"

"Can I take the shot and we can talk about that after?"

"Nope. You gonna want me on your film, cowboy"

"OK"

"How much?"

"100."

"Here's 20. It's public broadcasting."

"You're messin"

A hard look as she snatches the twenty.

"I'm Rategan"

"Angel."

Rategan knows this particular corner of Dundas and Sherbourne well, from directing a doc about private security companies. This is the drainpipe of all the city's effluence. The police have given up. There's so much booze, and drugs and hooking down here, if the cops responded to every brawl, every passed-out OD, every smashed window, they'd be down here 24/7. They've yielded the job of policing to a private security company called Irongarde. It's part of a North American trend, the privatization of policing. Deploying under-trained and under-paid "guards" to trouble spots. In their black shirts and billy clubs and walkie-talkies, their Rottweilers, "K-9's", they aim to intimidate.

Irongarde's owner scares the shit out of right-wing councillors with nightmare scenarios of rampant crime gangs and gets funding from the City to hire his uniformed thugs, at one-third the cost of the police. 3 for 1. Everyone wins, except the residents, who are racially profiled and bullied in a 24 hour manner the cops can't get away with.

It's amazing to Rategan that this kind of pig-headed, unlicensed law enforcement prospers in the heart of a nice liberal town like Toronto in the 1990s.

~~~~~~~~

He's intrigued by the footage he screens and goes back to the hood the next day and asks after Angel. He is told she's avoiding the cops at a room of a friend dying of AIDS in a charitable hospice. He finds her and makes a call to his best streetwise cameraman and asks if he can shoot Angel for one night - on spec. John Westheuser is the most effective disappearing shooter in the business. He rarely talks but he grunts. Could be Yes could be No. Hard to tell with John. They meet at the AIDS hospice, and it turns out they have to hide the camera to get in. The dying friend isn't there, but Angel is. She says she needs a 20 to get high before she can co-operate, so Rategan obliges. She scurries out to score some rock, comes back and smokes it. That metallic blue smell fills the bathroom, and she's giggling.

In the mirror, she puts on her make-up. She runs the mascara pencil over eyebrows mounded like a middleweight's. Her teeth have been busted up too, as has her jaw. The face powder covers the knife and razor and bottle flecks on her cheeks. And as she talks, her pitbull mug is transformed by pencil, paint and pad into a beautiful thing, alluring, humorous, promising and lustful.

She fires off clip after clip which John's camera devours.

They drive through her hood, Dundas and Sherbourne. Derelict housing, renos, the old Imperial Mansions, ugly apartment blocks, the shittiest little mall downtown. No Petulia Clark here, but Angel in the passenger seat, country music on the radio, singing along to Dolly and Patsy Cline; behind her, John shooting noiselessly and without respite. She yells out the window to her crowd.

Dealers.

"How much is that Drano shit you're selling tonight, Jama?"

"Fuck you, Angel."

Pimps.

"Go get a real job, asshole."

"Fuck you, you whore."

Johns.

A guy in a white pick-up.

"This doesn't get into that shitbox for less than a dime, buddy."

"Fuck you, then."

"Fuck yourself, asshole"

The Do-gooders.

"Helen. Any Snickers for me, darlin'?"

The vigilantes

"That bitch has been trying to get me barred for months"

"Clean up your condoms, Angel"

"Fuck you, Regina.. Is that a wig?"

This is the parade of the Underworld Queen.

Rategan thinks to himself that if someone doesn't pay him to make a film about this gal, he'll … make it anyhow.

In Canada where to get funding you have to get the idea past a committee of scaredy-cats who will dilute the shit out of your robust, brilliant ideas, its best to start shooting it on your own coin before The Grovel.

That's the Rategan M/O

More research, dozens of phone calls, and a bigger picture emerges of the intersection at Dundas and Sherbourne: it's a battleground for different urban visions.

Rategan shoots an interview with the right-wing owner of a B&B on the NW corner of the intersection who wants to bring in a massive pipe and suck all the scum into the sewers. Clean 'er up, disinfect, sandblast, plant rose bushes and garden gnomes.

Rategan and his partner Chris Sumpton cut the bits and bobs into a promo and, lo and behold, The National Film Board commissioner, Louise Lore takes one look and says:

"That's exactly the sort of film we should be making, folks!" and the money pours down.

The idea is simple. Take any intersection and examine the lives in the four sections. Dig in four directions. It could be a series. Four Corners. Take the bird's eye view.

It could be anywhere.. the Prairies, the Phillipines, Lagos. Especially Lagos. Wow. More characters than a Ken Russell movie.

Spend six months in any of them, and those characters will shine through, fighting, loving and suffering. You just need to get in there, get them to forget about the camera, and get the fuck out of the way.

Here, at Dundas and Sherbourne, the Four Corners read like this:

On the NW corner section, just above the Jazz Club on the corner, meet Regina Scheer, the monarchist owner of a B&B named Catnaps. Her balcony is festooned with little Union Jacks, and there's a cat face door-knocker. Inside is decorated with cat cozies, cat pillows, and a cat clock that meows on the hour. Regina is set on cleaning up the neighbourhood and is a driving force behind the pro-business Downtown Residents Committee. Preening, self-righteous Tories, most of them.

On the NE corner, OCAP, the Ontario Coalition against Poverty, led by a cockney firebrand named John Clarke. The Justice Maniacs. They believe in direct actions to find housing for the poor, and end homelessness. They will take Rategan along on various occupations of city hearings, empty housing sites, and welfare offices. A wild and fearless bunch, with every stripe of leftist fervour. Rategan, of course, is most partial to this mob.

On the SE corner, All Saints Anglican Church, opens it heart and its doors to the homeless with a free place to crash and free breakfasts.

On the SW corner the crack mart; a ratty little mall where the dealers and pimps and users hang out, tradin' and spasmin'.

It goes without saying that if you want to meet people you go to wherever they are, and you wait, until someone comes along and you start talking. Like fishing. You don't take the first one, or the second. Only someone from third onwards. Patience. He or she will walk into the role, like destiny.

Friday nights are always cooking so one night Rategan pays the third man, a dealer named Izzy to wear a wire. He then clambers up a fire escape opposite the mall to lie on the roof of the Jazz lounge with his camera and shoot the action. He already knows this will be his opening scene. Start on a chopper shot that stagger-moves from the glittering skyscrapers of Bay Street. A gravelly voiceover saying something like "Minutes from the glittering towers of Canada's multi-trillion dollar business district..." then the seeping sound of reggae, and the camera pans down to these shots Rategan is getting right now from the Jazz club roof. Then he'll cut to an ass-level walking shot behind a hooker as she slithers into the intersexion. Voiceover continues "... there hisses and crackles a seething hellhole of appetites run amok...(two-beat pause).. a neighbourhood at war." Ba-boom-bang.

Overwritten as usual but Rategan cannot resist a juicy syllable.

Through his earphones he can hear the howls and cries of the four corners picked up by the remote mike on Izzy's lapel. The cries for more. The cries of pain, cries of outrage, howls of insult and assault.

Look at my Canadian life; I'm dying in full sight.

Izzy is from Jamaica. He has had a face-freezing crackhead stroke rendering his heavy accent unintelligible.

His life is only about getting crack.

He'll smoke and be high for about 18 seconds, then the never-ending craving starts again. When Izzy had first started dealing in Toronto, he was a strong man from the island with no fear, driving a Chevy with a Selassie doll dangling from the rear-view mirror. But he can't stop breaking the number one rule of the dealer. Don't use.

Always owing, he starts cheating and stealing. The Chevy goes. Then, the stroke.

Rategan first meets Izzy next to a notorious mens' hostel around the corner, Seaton House.

Seaton House is the biggest homeless shelter in the city - occupancy 700, mostly men. The place is so bitter end, the caretakers have turned into prison guards, the milk of their human kindness all curdled.

Izzy has been barred from Seaton House for dealing. He takes Rategan behind the House to his rented room. It stinks like an armpit. The smell of poverty, the smell of someone who's given up and doesn't care. His doctor has told him if he doesn't stop smoking crack it will kill him. But he can't stop. He wants to die high and he's in a hurry. And nothing Rategan brings to the table is going prevent that.

What Rategan learns is that it's a free society in Canada, one of the freest in the world, and if you want to kill yourself on drugs, nobody is gonna stop you. There's no real public brake on suicide by drugs, quick or slow.

Angel, pursued by warrants and banning orders, has disappeared again.

There's a public housing apartment building west of the Jazz Club. Rategan finds her holed up in a room on the 14th floor with her new boyfriend, Dave the Goalie. Dave tells Rategan his story.

After an infancy from Hell, he was adopted by a farming family north of the city and had shown talent as a soccer goalie. By the age of ten he was the top net minder in Ontario, for his age. But as soon as he smoked his first joint he was a goner. Within months he's smoking and swallowing every drug he can get his hands on. Overnight, he becomes a thievin', lyin' druggie, stealing from his foster family and running away, again and again.

In their trashed room 1402, Dave and Angel are jonesing and planning their next hustle. Dave has been out the night before stealing copper wiring from construction sites, selling it, and they have already smoked the 40 dollars he's brought in. It's hot. He's wearing swimming trunks. She's wearing shorts and a tight halter-top, and she has a long fresh knife mark across her cheek below her right eye.

They explain the hustle. She'll take up her hooking spot on Sherbourne in front of Catnaps. Prime time is morning rush hour and mid evening.

"Morning rush hour?" Rategan asks.

"Yeah. Men who don't get laid have erections in the morning."

Her eyebrow arches as if there's something wrong about Rategan not knowing this.

"And in the evenings they get horny after a drink or two and before they get home to the missus who they can't stand anymore."

She chortles.

This is their hustle.

She'll pick up the john and point him down the blind alley. Just as she's getting him all fired up real good, Dave, who is hidden behind a garbage bin, will jump out, knife drawn, and they'll take the guy's money. Ninety percent of the johns will be happy to escape unscathed and won't call the cops. Those who do?

Angel admits to 123 criminal convictions. 123. How is that possible? Rategan thinks to himself. He checks with a contact with access to the database. She says, yeah. 122.

Assault, procuring, lewd acts, forgery, uttering death threats, assault with a deadly weapon. She is barred from entire neighbourhoods. It's a police procedure copied from New York City. You ticket troublemakers and get them out of bad areas. Angel is barred both from the intersection and barred from the building she is now in so the only way to get her out is in a blue recycling bin. She crams herself in and Dave slams down the lid and takes her down in the elevator. He wheels her over to the parking lot at Filmore's strip joint and as guilty-looking salesmen exit their brown Buicks for a quick lap dance, he tips her out. She rolls out like a burly Comâneci onto her toes, sticks the landing, and spreads her arms, grinning.

"Showtime."

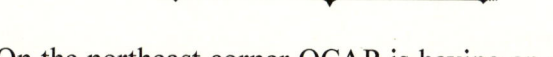

On the northeast corner OCAP is having an executive meeting. There's John Clarke and his sidekicks - the beatific Beric and the ultra-radical Suzi. There is also Gaetane, who weeps whenever he speaks about homeless people and finally Red, a youngster whose loathing for Rategan is something to be watched. Red is psychotic about "the media".

They are all cramped into a back office with two desks, festooned with placards from their "actions" and beneath a banner of Lenin leading the vanguard to glory. Rategan is trying to interview Clarke in the melee.

"So what are trying to draw attention to, through your actions?"

"To the genocide that 'as been unleashed on the poor and 'omeless population of this city. The fact of the matter is that someone dies every day on the streets of this city (exaggeration, surely, Rategan thinks) because of the policies of this 'artless government which reflects only the interests of the rich." [14]

"Yeah the rich" says Suzi as she fiercely adjusts her severe dark-rimmed glasses. She's the daughter of a top Conservative mandarin in Ottawa and was raised in tony Rockcliffe Park. She wields her sociology MA like a machete and looks about to explode.

"We are prepared to sacrifice our freedoms, our bodies for theirs."

Gaetan is tearing up. In an escalating whine he says "What they don't realize...the police when they act this way ... I mean... people are dying."

Clarke again - "Until such time as the city and all levels of government comes to grips with the crisis of 'omelessness and poverty, we will continue to confront them, in their banks, in their offices and yes, even in their homes."

'YESS" Red bursts, staring bug-eyed at Rategan, then cupping his meaty fist over the camera lens as Rategan twists on his pile of pamphlets to film him. "Don't shoot me. Don't ever shoot me", he growls.

"Then take your fucking hands off my camera.. or they'll be no documentary."

---

[14] Toronto Public Health reported that in 2022, 187 homeless died.

"So when's the next action?" Rategan asks Clarke.

"If you are vetted, we will let you know."

"Vetted? Vetted? What's this, the RCMP? I am not working for anybody else but myself and the National Film Board. It won't get any lefter than that in the real world, buddy. You won't get a more sympathetic hearing anywhere else."

They regard him, agape.

"Can I join OCAP? You say everyone is welcome."

Rategan attends a meeting of OCAP in the community center in the worst housing complex in Toronto. Every second Monday night, dodging the knots of drug and gun-toting Caribbean and Italian and Irish gangs and war-damaged Somalis bristling with random hostility, OCAP meets, open to all, to discuss how to bring down the state. It's a very Canadian way to seed a revolution.

The problem with OCAP is most poor people don't seem to want to follow them. They just want to survive their shitty jobs and low pay, keep their children out of jail or hospital and educate them enough to get a steady job.

But still, there's OCAP at it's corner looking out at the other three corners, disdainful of the religious salve that is the Anglican Church on its corner, avoiding any kind of judgement on the drug addicts and sex workers swarming all over the opposite corner, and targeting

Regina, and the gay realtors who are trying to turn filthy mansions into hugely profitable real estate.

Rategan has some difficulty setting up a meeting with the priest, Jeannie Loughrey, who has recently been installed as the incumbent of All Saints Church on the SE corner. She is clearly no publicity hog.

Rategan finds out she once worked for the CBC.

All Saints is a 19th century mid-sized church, where once the well-off families from nearby mansions worshipped. It is, during the cold weather months, now a dormitory for about 30 homeless people. The same sunlight slanting through the same stained glass angels on the rich of yesteryear, now pours grace and piety today onto the lumps of humanity breathing heavily in their blue, grey and red sleeping bags.

Next door the Community Hall is a food kitchen. Every morning and evening a team of volunteers with donated food feed a shuffling, wary lineup of fifty or sixty homeless.

When they finally meet, the Reverend Loughrey defensively asks. "What do you *want* of us?"

"Well. For starters. What is your theological obligation to the homeless?" Rategan replies.

"We will not judge them. This is a place of refuge, and sustenance. And we will continue to try and improve their situation, better our service to them. We want to make them feel safe, and loved. We are currently trying to get approval for a hostel for women who are particularly underserviced."

"Would you mind if I come in here to film occasionally?"

"Personally I would, yes."

Rategan is taken aback. He's never had pushback from a religious institution to film, including radical mosques in Iraq and Afghanistan, and a Serbian Orthodox priest who turned out to be hoarding weapons for his parishioners in the Croatian war.

"Why?"

"Written permission must be given by all parties. Some of these folks may not know the consequences of giving you their okay. There is a high incidence of mental illness, you know. And frankly I have more often than not found the media coverage of the homeless to be.... counter-productive."

"Didn't you yourself work for the CBC?"

"Precisely" she says, dead-eyed. "You come, you promise, you shoot, you leave, you stereotype, and you add to the victimization of the poor."

"Would you say that on camera?"

She looks at him, wordlessly.

Not Born Yesterday, he thinks.

Eventually, and reluctantly she agrees, and says her piece. Even, in one of the most moving scenes he ever films, she meets with Angel on the skids.

Rategan thinks she has that quality of steel mercy that is found in the Great Missionaries.

Rategan isn't allowed to film in the food hall, but he is allowed to help, to hang out. Which he does. The human experience may be more valuable than the filmed evidence.

He watches the men. Most seem strung out. He doesn't like the fact but he finds himself agreeing with the street cop who has told him the feeding program is a big obstacle to getting rid of the minority of bad actors at Dundas and Sherbourne. It sustains the bad and the good.

One day he spots a small wiry old man in a hurry stuffing bags with powdered mashed potatoes, soup, bread and cans. He is talking to himself. Rategan follows him out onto the street.

"Hey"

"Yeah?"

"What's your name?"

"Ed"

"Need a hand?"

"Sure, sure."

"Where are you going?"

"The Valley."

They lob his cache into the back of Rategan's van.

"Can you run a hundred meters with a railway tie on your shoulders?" asks Ed.

"Nope." Rategan laughs.

"Thattaway", he says, pointing to The Don River Valley.

They arrive at an abandoned playing field beneath a highway bridge. Ed gestures behind Rategan to the towering bridge over the Don River talking a mile-a-minute,. Rategan guesses the experts call this manic.

"Terrible, terrible. They fall from there. Terrible, terrible."

There'd been a rash of suicides off that bridge.

"Are you referring to the death last night?"

"Yes, another one. One every week. Terrible, terrible".

He arranges a yellow rope straight and parallel to a second rope which forms a wide lane for his run.

"I only do 75 yards nowadays, since I turned 70. But I am the only man in Canada who can run this in under 12 seconds carrying a weight like this."

He toes a thick length of wood. It looks like an old farmer's cattle yoke. There's a cold fall wind whipping across the track. Rategan gives Westheuser the "shoot" sign.

"You timing me?"

"Sure", says Rategan, who has already cued his stopwatch.

"Anytime, Ed."

The spindly old man puts the massive wooden yoke on his bony shoulders, totters a bit to get it balanced, then he's off!!

His little legs pump furiously, his trunk arched forward, his white hair flowing, and he runs the 75 yards at a fair lick.

It's an enormous feat of strength. Then to further impress, he tumbles the yoke off his shoulders to one side, drops chest down and does twenty pushups.

"What was my time?" he pants.

"12.8 seconds."

"Goddamn wind. Let me do it again."

"It's fine, it's fine. It doesn't matter, the time. It's incredible anyway."

"No fuckin way. I'm doing it again."

Rategan shrugs. But he gives Westheuser the cutting, "don't shoot" sign.

Ed drags the yoke down the track, humps it back on, and does it again. Halfway along, something on his right side seems to give way, but he keeps pounding along, his face getting redder, squealing with stress, until he bursts across his finish line and drops the yoke to the ground.

"14.8"

"Shit." He is panting mightily. Rategan hands him some water.

"I think I popped my Achilles again."

He invites Rategan for a cup of tea at his hovel, a mix of tent, corrugated asbestos, tires, concrete blocks, and blue and black plastic tarpaulins.

He tells a story of how he had been, in his day, one of the top sprinters in Ontario, how he had married his childhood sweetheart, and turned his family farm into a profitable gravel business. One day he had been out cycling Highway 7 and had been hit from behind by a truck. After a year in hospital, and with severe migraines, he emerged to a bankrupt business and a farm now controlled by a wife sinking slowly into alcoholism, divorce, a remarriage to a neighbour who taken over the farm, putting a severely impaired Ed out on the street.

Rategan knows he isn't going to use Ed in the NFB doc; too bizarre and eccentric; also away from the Four Corners. So he mentions Ed to a local reporter and he makes it onto CBC Toronto TV news, running bare-chested through a light snowfall, a wonder of toughness and longevity.

A good news oddity on a quiet day.

Six months later Ed is found dead in his shack, his head and ribs crushed by an axle that someone drops on him. Whoever has killed him has done it with emphasis.

Rategan gets a call from OCAP. An Action. 317 King St East. 12 noon. He drives down there.

OCAP has found a shuttered three storey building, owned by the Catholic Church, and OCAP demands that it immediately becomes a place to house the homeless.

Suzi is there leading the charge.

"No Justice!!" she cries.

"No Peace!!" answer the fifteen bedraggled protestors.

She orders a powerfully built street hombre to crowbar open the main door. Pop. Creak. Bang.

"No Justice, No Peace."

The punks are lovin' it. The Dykes are lovin' it. The ex-Cons are lovin' it.

Red is lovin' it too, though staring daggers at Rategan trying to catch it all on his Panasonic.

There are two other groups there - the cops and the racists.

One night Rategan goes on patrol with the two bicycle cops who are assigned to Dundas and Sherbourne. Kravchuk, a tall Ukrainian basketball player and Allison, a well-built, short Jamaican. They know all the ne-er-do-wells by their first names. They're based at 51 Division, which looks like a Stasi interrogation block plonked down in the heart of a public housing complex.

One hot Saturday afternoon in late August, Rategan goes there to interview the Superintendent, a barrel-chested man with a slightly off kilter nose, a hockey stick, no doubt. He is trying to find out what the strategy is towards the flotsam and jetsam of Dundas and Sherbourne but the Chief is a long-winded spout of cliché and low-key tolerance, as if he'd just come from a "New Initiatives" course. One of the worst interviews he's ever done with one of the most boring people on the planet.[1]

John Clarke has occupied the street outside the home of the Premier of the Province, Mike Harris, with an OCAP posse screaming "Murderer, Murderer!"

OCAP's chief funder, the Steelworkers union, has demanded they quit the tactic of confronting politicians in the homes or they may withdraw their support.

Rategan asks Clarke "Are you gonna apologize?"

"No. I want people to wake up. What we 'ave here is a crisis. A crisis of capitalism. The measures we take are directly proportional to the daily violence inflicted by Mike Harris's henchman on the poor and 'omeless of this city."

"What happens if the USW pulls its support?"

"We carry on."

The night they're filming the opening shot of the hooker walking down the rain-soaked sidewalk, Angel, despite promising blue in the face two nights previous, is nowhere to be found. Rategan figures she's in the clink or immobilized by drugs.

No Angel; but there is a First Nations hooker called Sherene. She doesn't look like much standing out there in the rain, all scrawny and drenched. But she's strangely magnetic. Sherene is never on the sidewalk for long. Rategan has seen the white boys in their juiced trucks pick her up and take 'er off. She had sliced Angel's arm in a fight over territory and Angel is jealous of her. With a racist lash.

"That little squaw, I'm gonna get 'er good one of these nights, O Boy, just watch me. Gonna slice that cunt up real good. Next time I see her I'm gonna kill her."

Sherene has been in homes and jails as long as she can remember. She's a cutter, flecked with knife scars. She twitches when she walks. Rategan figures she's on something very strong. Artane? Mandrax?

"Ok Sherene, this is 100 dollars if you get it right."

Gives her twenty and stuffs the rest into his back pocket.

"For later."

"I'm in." She smiles. For a millisecond. Not much to smile about in her life.

Westheuser is in place in the shadows next to her.

Through a Walkman Rategan plays Shereen the opening bars of Bob Dylan's "Love Sick" three times to get the cadence...

"Dum-dum-dum-

"I'm walking

Through streets that are dead

I'm walking

With you in my Head"

She has it.

"Let's do a rehearsal, Sherene. Go!"

He gives Westie the go sign.

She glides through eight yards of darkness, her hips rocking slowly, past the yellow light seeping out from the beer bottle windows of the jazz joint, through two more yards of darkness, into the harsh top light of the jazz joint entrance and out into the intersection like a fish spilling out of a net.

Whoosh.

Her slow hip-rock, her whole lower body becomes the engine of the Night, the beat of the doc. She is perfect. They shoot it three more times but that first take is the one they use.

"Is that all?"

"Sherene. You were perfect. A Star."

"So let's do more."

"That's all there is." he says, handing her the eighty.

"Shit."

A couple of weeks later when Angel emerges from jail and hears through the streetvine that Sherene got the 100 bucks earmarked for her she demands the hundred, with interest. In the First Base bar on Queen East, she jumps Sherene from behind and assaults her with a broken bottle. The First Nations kid is cut up awful, hospitalised. There are no witnesses and charges against Angel are not laid.

Back at The Four Corners chaos and anarchy erupts.

Someone has attacked Regina Scheer outside her B&B. The cops haul away two brawling street characters. One of them has been maced and an ambulance attends. OCAP is meeting across the street strategizing on how to fuck up a Prime Ministerial speech on Bay Street the next night. They decide this is an opportunity too good to resist. They pile out and it's full-on demo time. John Clarke jumps up on Rene's tidy faux Georgian balcony with its hanging fuchsia and declaims her as "Marie Antoinette-who-ate-cake-while-the-peasants-supped-gruel-and-were-tortured-to-death-by-a-police-state-spewing-the-toxic-products-of-outlawed-chemical-manufacturers-who-fund-right-wing-politicians-and-fascist-columnists," all sorts of mixed historical references in the ancient cadence of rage and righteousness, yeah down to the Middle Ages, but that it must stop here RIGHT HERE AT DUNDAS AND SHERBOURNE.

As he's winding down, Regina the Pitbull emerges and gut checks the skinny cockney into the arms of his stunned supporters below, on her perfect little lawn. She stands above him, hands on hips, like Tai Domi on a Saturday night.

At which point the Irongarde goons swarm in with their snarling Rottweilers, a TV cameraman takes a tumble, and finally, Superintendent Blair[15], the Great Dough Head, parts the seething crowd, megaphone in mitt, and calls for compromise and understanding. The Great Canadian Salve.

Two hours after it's started this most Torontonian of uprisings peters out in promises of meetings and memoranda. And Styrofoam garbage the only dead bodies lying about.

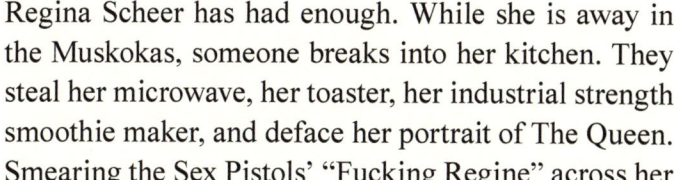

Regina Scheer has had enough. While she is away in the Muskokas, someone breaks into her kitchen. They steal her microwave, her toaster, her industrial strength smoothie maker, and deface her portrait of The Queen. Smearing the Sex Pistols' "Fucking Regine" across her smile.

"A thousand bucks worth", she screeches.

Angel offers her services to one of Regina's internet bridge friends from Minneapolis staying at the B&B. When he declines her services, she pulls a knife on him and snatches 50 bucks US.

She then wishes him a happy visit to Toronto.

---

[15] That Superintendent, William Blair, went on to become Chief of Police and a successful Liberal MP, and a senior cabinet minister in the Justin Trudeau government.

"For another ten bucks I'll tell you how to get to the CN Tower," she says, as he scrambles back to the B and B clutching at his pacemaker.

Regina storms out and there's an ugly confrontation with Angel, who retreats at the sound of a police siren.

"Stay away from my spot," says Angel

"You don't own this corner."

"Stupid Cunt" screams Angel.

"Crackhead Bitch."

Regina has balls, Rategan has to concede.

On the theory that eventually the boredom must break, Rategan films hours of the monthly meetings of the executive of the Toronto Downtown Residents Association. Chairperson, Regina Scheer.

One meeting is attended by the Municipal Councillor for the Area, Giles Somerville. Giles is a clean man. A very, very clean man. His eau-de-cologne precedes him into the room. His credentials and connections are impeccable and reach across all party lines, verily, into the offices of Premiers and Prime Ministers alike.

But he doesn't do dirty and so is never actually seen in the hood.

He and his executive assistant are "listening to all stakeholders".

But Somerville panders to the homeowners and regards the radicals as deluded zealots, eradicable pests, a marginally criminal fringe group.

"I will stand behind no one in my passion for the safety and security of all my constituents, whatever their identity or circumstances." A classic of Canadian political non-conviction.

He has a mega-plan. After a couple of weeks of LTAS[16] he unveils an ambitious solution for the Dundas and Sherbourne neighbourhood. It's called "Concept Horizon". The Holiday Inn has bought some land next to The Four Corners, and a 230-room hotel will be up and running in 18 months, a welcome addition to the Tourist boom.

The homeless? They will be offered public housing in the suburbs.

The addicts and petty thieves? There'll be a police sweep. Operation Zamboni.

The Church. Rein in by appealing to the Conservative Archbishop of Toronto.

---

[16] Listening To All Stakeholders

If there are any winners in a battle like East Side Showdown, it will always be the Giles Somervilles of the world. How this always works this way, puzzles Rategan. But he knows it's the dirty little secret at the heart of Canada's world-class democracy. The boring prevail.

After the Regina incident word gets around that Toronto Downtown Residents Association is performing a 24 hour surveillance job for the cops.

Out of the blue a cross-dressing prostitute, Keegan, is found murdered in an abandoned building where he'd turn tricks.

Tensions are running high.

It's late summer, the evenings are long, tempers short. The pimps and dealers let their mongrels snap at joggers and each other. Every night in the nearby park, Allen Gardens, there is a fight. Usually someone jonesing, wanting money owed or stolen. Wanting. Yelling. Exploding. Lou Reed is in the air.

"And the coloured girls go...

Too-to-doo-too-do-do-too....

The rest of Toronto is in a paroxysm of self-congratulation after being named one of the world's great cities by a New York travel Magazine.

Rategan attends to the bi-monthly OCAP meeting. By now, six months in, he has been accepted among them, his shooting forgotten.

And strangely enough the city establishment starts to view them as something of a conscience. At least somebody is doing something about all these rejects on the street.

Their meetings are salutary exercises in democracy. Clarke is the most democratic leader Rategan has ever seen in action.

Part of it is because Clarke and Heroux practice the art of coalition. OCAP is made up of several organizations. There's the wimmens' unit, the gays, the ex-prisoners, the mental patients, the union reps (steelworkers, public employees, postal workers, autoworkers), the radicals, the Trotskyites, the black flag anarchists, the communists, the Workers Revolutionary party, even a movie star trying to find her truth, and a lone Greek Communist. There's an agenda, laid out by Suzi, the fire-breathing daughter of the Mandarinate. Rategan has heard that her Dad runs executive meetings with an iron rod at the Department of the Solicitor General, in Ottawa. She sits there in her paint-spattered farmer's overalls, white shirt, work boots and those glasses. Scraggly black-brown hair. No matter how severe she looks she can't disguise how sexy she is. Just coiled energy. Right now it's serving the revolution. She's formidable, capable of instantaneous vision and acts of courage. Moving before others think.

There are four things on the agenda that night. They're upstairs at the Regent Park Community Centre above the security guard hangout and the single mom support groups and the T'ai Chi and ESL classes and the dealers in the playground outside.

"We have to be out by 11," says Suzi, glancing over her glasses like a member of the Central Committee. She would have shot the Romanovs in a heartbeat, Rategan thinks.

The big item is the rallies at the private homes of their opponents. They had gone to the Premier's house, infuriating everyone. "No JUSTICE No Peace", while he's trying to watch The Masters on a quiet Sunday afternoon. Rategan sympathizes. Invasion of Privacy. Rather like Eviction. All OCAP's funders have been asked by Queen's Park to end their support.

Everyone gets to speak. Every group. Clarke patiently listens to each and every submission. Everyone is for it. Home invasions.

The last guy to speak is Gus, the septuagenarian Greek Communist, an explosive guy, thickset. On every issue his speech is the same and it goes like this, in very rough English -

"I don't know what this is so much but I can tell you, when the people rise up the fascist crush down they have no heart they kill my sister my brother my father, against a wall, bang bang the whole village, and the working people must fight back to defend their lives, everywhere the imperialists are crushing the poor people but the poor people are like the rock!"

The fist springs up. All fists rise.

"Long Live Greece Viva EAM ELAS, VIVA PSARROS ".. and he breaks into body-wracking sobs. Same thing, every time, whatever the topic at hand. Unflappable Clarke says -

"Thank you Gus. We respect and value the experience you have of this. Thank you for your inspiration, thank you." And two or three people clap, briefly.

"Who's next?"

"Prisoners rights."

And so on until all the disparate groups have thrown in their heartfelt portion of righteous rage.

At the end Clarke skillfully and accurately summarizes each submission, laying out the OCAP view and they vote on something with Suzi rushing them to finish by 11, as a cleaner stands at the door, broom ready.

On a couple of occasions Red stands up and accuses Rategan of being a CSIS informer. Clarke explains that the majority had already voted to let him sit in as part of his film to show exactly how OCAP operates. You will never find this in any cabinet or council or corporation in the country Rategan thinks.

Rategan has also earned their trust by showing up at their actions, filming them and helping out.

In the occupation of the King Street building there is a melee between some homeless demonstrators and a neo-Nazi raiding party of three. A plainclothes cop is cut on the scalp. More blood than damage, but a First Nations guy, one of the OCAP homeless, is hauled off and charged with assaulting a police officer. Moose, as he is called, has such a long record he doesn't have a prayer, until Rategan hands to the defence team his footage, which clearly shows the undercover man getting clipped by the knuckle-duster on the fist of a whaling neo-Nazi.

The case against Moose is withdrawn.

One Thursday, Rategan is coming back from his weekly golf game to his office when he gets a call from Suzi that they are occupying a welfare office. Federal Government property. A single mom, an undocumented refugee with a sick kid, has been turned down for emergency welfare and she's brought her case to OCAP.

Rategan grabs his Panasonic and arrives just in time to join eight OCAPers walking in. Security men wheel about, awaiting instructions. Clarke makes a real peach of an impromptu speech. They are not leaving until Marie Sarrasto is given her $280. Everyone sits down. Thereafter follows long-distance phone calls.

The staff glare at Rategan, who has told the vice-chairman of administration that he is doing a documentary for the NFB about OCAP. These are the days before the world turns against the crusading filmmaker. Michael Moore hasn't even made his first million. Rategan hangs in with the welfare office occupiers for six hours until some suit comes down from somewhere and announces that Maria gets her money.

This happens to OCAP *all the time*. Many of the buildings they occupy are sold to public housing and turned into homes for the homeless. Medical services are extended to people who live on the street. An Out Of The Cold Program is established at the church, run by the weeping Gaetan. Beric washes the feet of the poor every Thursday. Rategan sees his eyes water up as he does it. The essence of devotion. The ennobling business of ministering to the needs of the poor.

A story is published on Toronto's successful policies towards the homeless, incorporating the relentless activism of OCAP. John Clarke is labeled "a Cockney Robin Hood."

But words are cheap.

In reality, they are harassed for their efforts. Their leaders are arrested, spuriously charged, and detained in jail. And they can't apply for any financial support without alarm bells going off.

In a crackdown right out of the apartheid playbook, Rategan notes, John Clarke is banned from addressing any public gathering. He has to wear an ankle bracelet for eighteen months. He is restricted to his home and the cramped OCAP office. One windy night on the Don River Bridge, above Ed the Runner's track, a couple of fun-loving cops stop him and bend him over the ledge for a laugh.

When all the footage is in, and backed by the exquisite patience of the NFB, the documentary comes together like a Faulkner novel. It makes an impact. It's nominated for the only award that matters to Rategan, The Donald Brittain, named after a legendary NFB filmmaker who he had met, half-cocked, at an Ottawa reception.

Faced with this golden opportunity to extract advice from a master, Rategan had asked Brittain what the three most important qualities of great documentary-making were.

"Tell me what you are going to tell me."

"Tell me."

"Then tell me what you just told me."

After the film is screened, he has a coffee with Clarke; who is unimpressed by the film.

"You made us out to be right, but losers."

Regina and her allies, the Reverend Russell, Irongarde and the cops -

Nobody in the film liked it, or the way they were portrayed.

In a perverse and probably self-justifying way, Rategan sees that as a success of sorts.

The film shows that poverty cripples. Sex is a transaction. And apartheid's bag o'tricks are universal.

The shock to Rategan is that the tactics of fascism are merrily deployed here in inner-city Canada. The trick is to persuade people, if challenged, that there are some behaviours by the poor and marginalized that justify the use of fascist techniques. To maintain the peace for all the millions of hard-working, law-abiding, though tax-dodging Torontonians.

And even in this dark scenario, character rises through the murk, from all sides, to sing its insistent song.

xxxxxxxxxxxx 30 xxxxxxxxxxxx

DOCUMENTARIES:

"In Security" Cogent/Benger Productions. Hot Docs 1998 nominee best political/social issue documentary

"East Side Showdown" NFB/CBC Witness. Donald Brittain Gemini Awards 1999 nominee best social/ political documentary.

"a remarkable 1998 doc (made by Robin Benger) about an area of Toronto, and the awful ironies of urban existence.... This is formidable, provocative television." John Doyle. Globe and Mail.

6 RATEGAN DOES MANDELA

Rategan lives in apartheid South Africa since arriving from England at the age of 10 and instinctively loathes the way the black majority is treated. Before he understands what it is and how it works, he knows something evil rules the land. His revulsion is fuelled by some of the best journalism he'll ever see, as the English-language papers compete to report as graphically as possible the latest apartheid obscenity: farmers using bull whips on the potato-pickers of the Orange Free State, leaving them to die; dogs and hoses attacking naked black prisoners in Johannesburg's Old Fort, surreptitiously photographed from a nearby roof.

His group, white upper-class English-speaking northern suburbs Johannesburgers, never soil their hands with this kind of direct brutality. His group makes excuses for its complicity.

"It's the Afrikaners. It's their fault, not ours.

Their underlying view is that "the blacks aren't ready yet. If they don't keep them down, it could all blow up overnight."

Standing in the sunshine, amid the servants, swimming pools, tennis courts and verdant gardens, the Anglos are privately thankful for Afrikaner nationalist rule. It leaves them to make money in the sunshine

"Beats Birmingham every time."

Rategan is ripe for a way that leads to the end of the racist horror of the nation.

At Wits University he meets a few others of his generation who feel the same way. They who oppose apartheid form a sort of secret society, conversing so that they cannot be overheard, as the organisations and leaders who came before them are silenced, banned, jailed, or dead.

At seventeen, he is arrested and put in a jail cell in South Africa, a two-day experience which gives him a fleeting idea of what life is like on Robben Island for Mandela and the other political prisoners, in for life. One element of it, he learns, is that one is completely at the mercy of the security police.

At the age of twenty, he is expelled from South Africa, and comes to Canada. He works on beer delivery trucks and in the nickel mines, ending up working at the Canadian Broadcasting Corporation for twenty years.

He is privileged to learn from the masters of the craft of documentary storytelling, how to shape narratives about every subject in Canada and around the world. In making dozens of documentaries he imagines a viewer, an inquisitive ten-year-old child somewhere in the far reaches of Canada and beyond, watching, learning, on the lookout for guidance. Suddenly he is safe, and radio and television dissolves all borders. It is the way ahead.

He sees other people and networks tell the story of Nelson Mandela and thinks how wonderful it would be if he could do that some day. After sitting on his 58-page proposal for a year, Mark Starowicz at the CBC's documentary unit delivers that opportunity.

Rategan starts out with the conviction that Mandela is some kind of God, and it is his destiny to tell that story, while disguising his adulation. Of course adulation is the kiss of death for any biographer. Adulatory biographies should be thrown out within the first five minutes. Fans cannot be trusted. One needs objectivity. But as Rategan finds out, something about him, something deep, dark and cynical keeps intruding on his worship of Mandela and his wife Winnie. So in the making of the following tribute, one is constantly thrown by the negativity expressed by Rategan. The contradictions about commercialism, his strange penchant for celebrities, and, in Winnie's case, the paradox of a beatific Mother of the Nation dooming informers to a grisly death.

Rategan starts out wanting to frame the story about Nelson Mandela for that ten-year-old. See here, there *is* a way to overcome great loneliness and marginalisation brought on by racism; to bring freedom and justice and liberation to millions. Because that's what Nelson Mandela has done.

Making him, arguably the Greatest Political Leader of the Twentieth Century.

NOVEMBER 17, 2003.

Prelude

Rategan is in London, on his way to South Africa. In an hour he'll be interviewing Anthony Sampson, Mandela's official biographer. In 1951 Sampson, an Oxford man, travelled to South Africa to work as Editor of the biggest black newsmagazine there, *Drum*, meeting and befriending Mandela before he was sent to jail.

Rategan has his list of questions, in chronological order, that will, he hopes, evoke revelations. The trick is to ask short, open-ended questions that press the right buttons. Release the flow, the expertise within the other, insight based on experience. With Sampson, Rategan wonders why he hasn't been in other Mandela documentaries. His biography of Mandela is absolutely one of the best political biographies written on anybody. And he is a great yarn-spinner.

In Parliament Square Brian Kelly and he are filming the Smuts statue.

There's a black and white picture of Mandela standing here from his secret trip to the UK in 1962. Rategan looks up at Smuts, the bantam striding against the grey sky, and he wonders if Mandela, back then, envied him, thinks, he doesn't deserve to be there, I do. And does he think that one day he will?

NOVEMBER 22, 2003

At Heathrow catching his flight to South Africa Rategan bumps into an old school friend going the other way. At school Stefan Dalton-Smith and he were close friends. They were both prefects, both on the victorious rugby team, boys playing together every holiday in the veld and in the swimming pools and on the tennis courts of the suburbs north of Johannesburg.

After school they had gone separate ways. Stef into compulsory military service, then to law and business school, and a highly successful career running one of Africa's biggest management consultancies, which he owns.

Rategan ducks military service, thanks to his British citizenship and a little white lie he tells at his recruitment hearing, something about going to Oxford the day after high school finishes.

"What the hell?' Rategan says, and hugs him.

"Rategan!"

"What are you doing here?"

"I'm on my way to Geneva for some meetings about business post-apartheid"

"High-level stuff, hey?"

"And you?"

"I'm going out to make a film on the life of Mandela."

"Fantastic. You live in Canada now, yeah?"

"Yes. Wife, three kids. How about you?"

"Married. Two kids"

He is impeccably dressed in tailor-made shirt and jacket, still athletic, dashing.

Rategan is wearing his foreign correspondent gear, khaki shirt, safari boots.

"What do you think is going to happen?"

"Mandela is unimpeachable, a God. Our worry is how long he can last: and whether the blacks will fuck it up as soon as he goes."

Rategan imagines who the "our" refers to.

"You should come back, run SABC."

"I actually applied! Never heard back."

Dalton-Smith sniffs.

"Probably better set where you are. Listen, call me and we'll have lunch. I'll be back next Wednesday."

He hands Rategan his card: "SDJ Consulting", and a phone number.

Rategan is sardine-canned into the flight to Johannesburg, and despite taking yet another Immovan, has a sleepless seven hours.

His team for South Africa is Luc Savard, an irascible but perfectionist cameraman; Musa Radebe, a lovable, street-wise soundman from Soweto, irrepressible; Charlene Smith, connected, hyper, his Johannesburg-based fixer; his sister Ann Thomas, a super-efficient production manager; and Mxolisi "Welcome" Ngozi, his old friend, a child of Soweto, a multilingual charmer.

DECEMBER 7

This morning at 6.45 they knock on the door of Albie Sachs's flat in Melrose. A sunny art-enhanced room, palm trees painted on one wall and a wooden coelacanth among the African sculptures. Rategan is severely hung over

Albie goes and fetches coffee. His eyebrows are still flecked with minuscule fragments of shrapnel from the bomb that should've killed him in the 1980s. He delivers. A just man, with a sweeping humanitarian view. Majestic insights into Mandela. Everyone respects Albie. Rategan loves him.

One interview done.. dozens to go.

CHRISTMAS IN QUNU. MANDELA'S HOME.

His new house stands alongside the main East London-Mthatha highway. Mandela had asked an architect Rategan knows to design a house based on the prison warder's cottage he lived in during his last year of captivity. A roomy suburban house has been added to this bungalow design.

All the children of the area, about three thousand of them, are assembled on a hill above Mandela's place to receive presents from The Leader.

The previous year, with Oprah Winfrey at his side, the event attracts an out-of-control crowd of fourteen thousand grasping kids. This year, security fencing has been set up enclosing a five-acre site, police and private security are out in force, choppers buzz about, one disgorging the obnoxious cockney boss of.

The kids are broken into about nine groups and assembled around the bases of six platforms, on which cavort a truly appalling collection of idiotic corporate mascots.

Eight-foot-high peanuts, candy bars, soft drinks and crisp products improbably hip-hop above the gawping rural children, the crass choreography of consumerism. This is the lesson of 27 years in prison fighting apartheid. A bag of chocolate peanuts?

A DJ whips up a frenzy as Mandela approaches in his motorcade. He is driven to the head of the throng in a black-windowed BMW, so that when he emerges in a characteristically brilliant shirt, it's like a butterfly from a dark chrysalis. The mothers cry out, dance and ululate ecstatically.

Mandela's body is rigid with age. Burly aides support him. A white girl lunges out of the crowd and tries to embrace him; she is repelled, rugby-wrenched away by his security team. "Can't I just hug you, please?", she cries out plaintively.

Rategan's cameraman gets in close as Madiba is elbow-guided to a small seating dais with three chairs. The cacophony around him is ear-splitting -- screaming children, pounding speakers and the DJ hollering: "Our Liberator, Our President, Our Father, please give a huge Happy Christmas welcome to Madiba..."

It reminds Rategan of the Dance of the Dictators. He's seen it with Mugabe, Moi and Nujoma. Screeching, amplified adoration.

Mandela knows the importance of reaching the children, of giving them some special joy, an eternal memory on Christmas Day, transcending the tackiness. Any dance for the king, and noise for a living god ...

Mandela has a distinctive gesture. His smile is one of the great smiles of all time, so broad, almost muscular. A smile carved out of the granite of monstrous suffering and endless patience. But then he wipes his huge paw down over the smile to assume the grim mask that is his expression most of the time. Easter Island immobile.

It reminds Rategan of a documentary he did on George Foreman, the American heavyweight who smouldered at him with homicidal intent until the little red light on the camera went on. Then transformed, Foreman beamed and cajoled and played America's cuddly bear. Or like the Queen, that grim, set expression, then the illumination of her smile, then gone. The mega-famous look unapproachable and tightly in control of all the dark forces, until that fleeting ignition of joy for the masses.

But this man, who he has been in close proximity to several times in both Canada and South Africa, is the embodiment of justice, of leadership, of humaneness. Everything one can learn about him, from the very early days of crippling rural poverty here in the Transkei, through to the moment he stands at the podium at the birth of the New South Africa and through to now, and every day to his death, everything is beyond reproach. Jesuitically, he lives for others. His own personal life story is full of death, loss, tragedy, treachery, danger and deprivation. Yet because he has seconded himself so, because he has lit the path from darkness and despair to freedom and the light he is immortalised. And Rategan hews to him. Rategan has read his every word. Rategan in Mandela has found a person worth revering. Praise him! Praise him to the heavens! Study, study his life!

Suddenly Rategan realises Mandela, a few feet away, is beaming at him. With the smile that can raise an entire continent. And Rategan smiles back.

"I see you," he thinks. And Mandela is replying "I see you."

Later there is a lunch for the commercial sponsors of the event, which they are invited to. There Rategan gets as close to Mandela as he ever will. Mandela invites sponsors, and other guests to his raised table and one by one they get a handshake and a word.

Rategan joins a line with the Sopranos from Wonder Bread Company, the Fat Boy from The Mandela Museum, and burping tourists from Belgrade. This is his chance to ask the man himself for the one-on-one interview he's been lobbying for over months. Come his turn and Mandela grasps Rategan's hand in his right hand.

"Welcome, welcome."

"I'm actually from Canada and I'd like to convey Christmas greetings from the millions of Canadians who consider you to be their favourite citizen."[17]

"Oh, I see." he says.

His eyes are crinkled and focused on Rategan's.

"Thank you, thank you" he envelopes Rategan's hand with his other, great pillowed hand.

Rategan looks deep into his berry-brown eyes and makes the connection, and is about to mention the reason-I'm-here-is-to-get-an-interview, but Mandela asks: "And how is your Prime Minister?"

It knocks Rategan off balance. A critical pause. He is already conscious of the next person in line.

"We have a new one now. Mr Chretien has been replaced by a Mr Paul Martin," he hears himself say.

"Oh, I see. Well please give him my regards." and then, with the gentlest of gestures, moves Rategan along. Rategan is now facing his wife, Grača Machel, she laughing at the fact he has come all the way from Canada, here, to Qunu.

He's blown it.

---

[17] In 2001 Mandela received honorary citizenship from Canada.

Boxing Day.

Staying on the coast in rondavels by the beach, Rategan has a sleepless night ruing the opportunity missed when he shook Madiba's hand.

"I'm doing a documentary. Could we interview you?" That's all he needed to say.

It would have taken five seconds. Instead, like some minor state functionary, he conveys fraternal greetings from the People's Republic of Canada. As if he's Canadian enough to offer that anyway.

He gets up.

As the sun breaks over the Indian Ocean, they fly over the corrugated roads the hour and a half to Madiba's highway mansion. He drives right in. Gets out. The front gate is still swinging on its hinges. A Nice Young Man tells him Madiba just drove off to catch a flight back to Maputo. 15 minutes ago. Rategan's heart sinks.

He has a letter for him. Nice Young Man gestures to the mansion, to take it to "Mimi".

He walks into Nelson Mandela's home.

A small office tucked to the right of a hallway reveals a round faced young woman with a beatific smile and warm manner. Mimi.

"You just missed him."

A young man walks in.

"Hi!" he says

"Hi! And you are?"

"Indaba."

"Indaba Mandela? Grandson?"

"Yes."

"Nice to meet you. I'm Rategan Edwardes. I'm doing a documentary film. Can I talk to you?"

"Sure," pointing to one of the cavernous rooms, "I'll be in there."

Mimi promises to get Rategan's grovelling letter to Madiba, but his hopes waver when she says that means it will be faxed to Mandela's office in Johannesburg, to Zelda.

Zelda la Grange. Mandela's gatekeeper, Mevrou Nee[18]. The name is the sound of a slamming door. He has had multiple fruitless contacts with the immovable Zelda, a strongly built Afrikaans girl Mandela had plucked out of the government typist pool in the President's office in Pretoria.

---

[18] Madame No

A stroke of genius. A born and bred Afrikaner from Pretoria. Placing a daughter, one of theirs, in centre frame. Defanging the Boer. But in her own way, intimidating, like a Springbok rugby lock guarding his captain.

The optics are perfect for that white section of the population most traumatised by his election victory. Mandela reassures the Afrikaners by celebrating the Rugby World Cup win, wearing a Springbok jersey, keeping a few in the Cabinet, charming the elderly widow of the architect of apartheid, Betsy Verwoerd, over a cup of tea, and keeping Zelda at his elbow at every public appearance. She is good at it.

Rategan thanks Mimi, and shakes her warm hand.

Instead of turning out, he turns in, following the muted sound of boom-ka-boom hip-hop until he finds Indaba, earphones around his neck, eating breakfast at ten.

Eggs, bacon, mushrooms, toast, tomatoes, on a glass table, the tinted, one-way windows looking out over the Qunu valley of Mandela's boyhood.

Indaba has a sweet, droll, long face, more that of his grandmother, Mandela's first wife, Evelyn, the nurse, "the sweet country girl", the Jehovah's Witness who left him during the terrorising times when Mandela was charged with sabotage.

Indaba tells Rategan he is taking three courses at Damelin College, a place one goes to catch up on failed high school subjects. Rategan had been there in the '60s, when it looked like he was going to fail Afrikaans matric. They agree to meet in January and do an interview about the legacy of Mandela.

He leaves with farewells to Mimi and a chat to the guy at the gate – who in fact, turns out to be a king-in-waiting, the grandson of Jongintaba, the royal that saved Mandela from a life of grinding, nameless poverty.

He offers to take them to the Royal Place of Mqekwhezeni. It's a critical phase in Mandela's life, and Rategan thinks he can build a scene there. He tells Rategan he takes care of the all the staff at Mandela's home. But Madiba won't be back until next Christmas, he says.

They drive past the field where the children played. The ground is strewn with hundreds of discarded free breakfasts, styrofoam containers, their contents of baked beans and synthetic wieners half-eaten in the hot dirt.

Cleaners in orange overalls speckle the hillside. There is a clump of 500 women. Today, it's food packages for the parents, he says. Even though Mandela has flown.

After forty minutes of banging on rocky dirt roads a valley is revealed and they are there: the Cradle of Greatness.

Everything is still, save for the humming of heat, insects, birds, the occasional bleat of a goat or yelp of playing children. Luc the cameraman captures the beauty of this. The absence of music, canned carols, the cacophony of Christmas far from these soft hills.

They shoot the place where the fatherless Mandela grew up. It is beautiful beyond the writing of it.

There's a boy, Mandela's great-nephew, with exactly the same features. The strong brow, the broad cheekbones, the slanted eyes. He stands in for Mandela, under the huge council tree, bang in the middle of the village square. They even find an old army coat that stands in well for the one Mandela wore as a boy in this very spot seventy-five years before. Rategan's luck. Rategan also has the excerpt of Mandela's telling of it in his head, and they shoot that. His autobiography, *Long Walk to Freedom*, is the Bible of this shoot, and Rategan has about sixteen critical moments memorised to the last syllable.

They spend a couple of hours there.

When they are done, Rategan walks off on his own and stands in silence, his eyes slowly covering every yard. Hillside, dirt road, wooden fence, vegetable patch, dam, the valley ahead, the low hill, the grazing cattle. The insects whirring, birds swerving.

Rategan loves deeply the absence of things. The South African boy is back in him, with the light, the dust and there's a prickling behind his eyes. Regret. A battle abandoned, just when he most understood it all. Not much use in freezing Toronto.

But it only lasts as long as the next decision. To leave. The prince has a face he would serve in a heartbeat. Rategan pays him one hundred rand for all of them and the prince is very grateful and dignified.

"Of all the people who have come here to take pictures you are the first to offer this. Thank you very deeply."

Rategan hears this with mixed gratification. The warm touch, the stroked hand on the slippery slope.

Later, they film real initiates getting the speech that Chief Meligqili (Mxolisi) gave Madiba at his circumcision ceremony in 1934. Welcome delivers, in a strong, gusty wind, his words lacerating the cloudless sky. Rategan can see the incredulity on the faces of these initiates. Thanks to Luc and Musa and Mxolisi, this will work.

HOLE-IN-THE-WALL, DECEMBER 27TH

It is Rategan's first day off. He decides to kick the smoking and walk nine kilometres up the Wild Coast to a village where he has booked a massage. It is a breath-taking walk.

In each bay there is the high path and low path. The high path traverses grassy hills thirty stories high, a quarter moon beaten over a thousand years by millions of feet and hooves. The low route is quicker, more direct through sand, rocks and cliffsides.

A bit weary after climbing up and over on the high paths, Rategan sizes up the long, curved bay, and takes the low route. Halfway along the low path, the rocks jut out into crashing waves. It's called the Wild Coast, a death trap for seafarers, with powerful currents and unsailable winds.

Spotting a pathway over the corner of what seems like a manageable, low cliff he heads upwards, increasingly finding the footholds difficult: better for goats and crampioned climbers than a 52-year-old two-hundred pounder with spikeless golf shoes.

He finds himself trapped. Neither able to proceed further upwards nor go back. Looking down, he suddenly realises a slip would result in a fifty-foot tumble, broken limbs at least, or worse. The rock and the skull.

He fingers his cell phone and figures if he is still conscious he wonders if he can rustle up a chopper in 30 minutes, but his levity soon chills with the memories of a hundred bad dreams about exactly this sort of terrifying situation. The fact that he has had this dream so often convinces him that it is finally, actually going to happen. That stunned dark ringing skull-thump and then … blood in the shallows.

He is stuck on a cliff alone above a crashing ocean. He cannot go forward or back. Whenever he moves, his shoe slides, and shale cascades down the cliff and shatters on the rocks below.

A beautiful place to die, no doubt, but he does have a family to serve, love and sustain and, above all, a documentary to finish, the documentary of his career, the blueprint of a life to inspire millions worldwide. Albeit, so far, without a Mandela interview. People who know Rategan would dismiss very rapidly any suggestion that he had thrown himself off the cliff because he had failed to get his man. And this is not the time to remind himself that a hundred other documentary filmmakers could do the film. He is not irreplaceable. There might be that end note: Rategan Edwardes 1951-2003.

For the next five minutes he is seized with terror. Convinced any move will send him plunging. He clings, unmoving, to the cliff.

Eventually, inching his way back down he manages to gain a foothold on a rock ledge, but as he twists his body to plant the other foot, he slips on a rivulet of water and bounces down, gravity released, *thwump*, tearing skin off his clutching arm, banging his neck and nose, but coming to a thudding stop on the broad back of a vast rock, the last one above the waves. A thirty-foot drop.

He lies there, trembling, thinking of his dead nephew Rupert, his dying father, his cancerous sister, the blue sky, the sounds of life, gulps of life and breath, thankful to be alive. He decides he won't tell anyone about this.

He won't. If he were to read about someone else doing it, he would say: "What an idiot. Lucky bugger."

It's the truth. It happened in this paradise. Where Millions of lives have been snuffed out by no education. No doctors here. But it produced Mandela, tough as this Rock.

It's not the *Man* himself any more. It is the body of work that has been launched from the body of The Man.

"This life have I given that you may be free."

Amen.

Back at the rondavels[19], a place called Hole-in-the-Wall, mostly Afrikaans families on Christmas hols, there's an urgent message for Luc. His partner, in Ottawa, has been badly injured in a car accident. The cameraman has to go home, on a sixteen-hour flight. For a week. They take him to Mthatha airport for his trip back to Canada.

Welcome and Rategan then drive to Madiba's birthplace, Mvezo, smoking *skyfs*[20] all the way, picking up hitchhikers, shooting the strange abandoned spot where Mandela first saw the light of day.

---

[19] Round traditional African dwelling places.
[20] Small dagga-speckled joints.

The Mbashe River winds in meandering U-shapes against a low clff where Mandela the child climbed and played. The place his father smoked himself to death, expiring finally from emphysema. His father never had access to a doctor.

On the way back to the highway, they pick up an old Xhosa man and his nephew wrapped in a thick blanket, chalk on his face. He is an initiate, in agony, as his circumcised penis has become infected. Often they use serrated knives and cast the initiates out into the bush to fend for themselves for forty nights. Infections like this are fairly common. They drop the two at the hospital.

He gets a message. Ahmed Kathrada, so close to Mandela, during the uprisings, and for 29 years in jail with him, reneges on an interview he'd promised weeks before.

"I can't do it", he says, over the phone. "What do you mean you can't do it?" Rategan pleads.

"I just can't. They are all the same"

Kathrada now joins Tutu, Ramaphosa, Magubane, Mandela (N and W) and Mbeki as turndowns. There's a pattern here. They are all black. The A-list. They've all been asked by every news outlet on the planet.

Rategan wonders if Kathrada would have done it for a few hundred dollars. And whether it says something about the status of Canada.

In Cape Town, Rategan's father is also dying of emphysema. He stands over his thin, sweating body. The nurse tells Rategan the doctor has said he has lost 95 percent of his lung capacity. His father wants a cigarette. When Rategan refuses, he glares at him with his fixed yellow-stained eye, which says: "I raised you and this is what you do to me?"

ADDICTION

Leaning against the door, Rategan's mother, addled with Alzheimer's, smiles wanly.

They are both in a retirement village. Separate rooms after sixty years of marriage. Stunned.

She keeps asking.

"What are we going to do about Father?"

Rategan doesn't tell her.

Nothing.

Percy Faith on the tannoy.

The truth is, of course, like the many dogs and horses she put down, he needs to be put down. Instead the body of this brave, successful man heaves involuntarily, sucking humiliation, pain and consequences out of the air.

Rategan has taken care of his affairs. He can go any time.

Now his sister, his SA production manager, comes down with ovarian cancer; his father is dying of emphysema; his mother is being driven down by Alzheimer's. He is at the centre of three breaking lives and the only one he cares about is Mandela, to whom he is not even related.

CAPE TOWN

He is waiting in the van outside their hotel. Kids watch from the shadows at the far side of the square, puffing up plastic bags and sucking them in, sniffing glue. Nine-year-old kids ...

(At a walkabout in Cape Town shortly after his release, the street kids swarm Mandela. He stops and speaks to them. After thinking about it, he decides to donate $150 000 of his own money and challenges others to do the same. In this way was started the Nelson Mandela Children's Fund.)

Rategan looks at one boy, eight going on eighteen, and pleads with his expression. He looks back at Rategan, stone-body against a tree, head cocked to one side, a sweet smile, a come-on.

Rategan shakes his head, says "No! No! No! Don't do this!" cold bony body in a doorway in winter.

The shoot is on hold. His cameraman has returned to Ottawa to be with his injured lady, and they are eyeless until his return. A crew without a camera. When Luc does get back, on January 7, they are interviewing and recreating ten hours a day. In the middle of a Robben island cell recreation shoot of Mandela receiving the telegram of his son's death, his cell phone rings.

It's the chief nurse from his father's home.

He hears the word "emergency" before the phone dies.

"Which tie? The brown or the red?"

"A sherry decanter for the Botha meeting?"

"Smoke machine down!"

The actor practises a fall onto the bed.

"SSSSSSHHHH!!"

"Rolling!"

And there's an emergency with his dying father.

Evenings north of the city only Dad ever enters. The cicadas and hadedas and cooing pigeons, the blue gum smells, occasional soft gust rustling the leaves, the dogs half asleep, eyes on the pathways beyond the gate.

Two huge trees positioned a goalpost apart in their spacious front lawn and his father, still in tie and braces from the office, chipping crosses for Rategan to nod in at the far post.

The sun always. Always the sun.

"Get on with it. Off you go!"

The English in Africa.
Chip, float, bouff.

Pass back.

Chip, float, bouff.

The bevelled whisky glass, the packet of Rothmans, the ones with the blue label. The faux-Etonian radio commercials, jet flights to foreign lands to smoke with old war pals, to reminisce about Palestine, the Battle of Britain, the bombing runs. Rothmans, see the world, have a drink, Simone Signoret in the moonlight, Coward on the gramophone.

Smoke rising in the place at the footpath's end.

The English in Africa.

The Sword and the Cross, and the Gold.

The Portuguese cut their hands off.

The Germans massacred.

We the British, velvet racists.

Philemon, the servant. Sweet, but in another world. "The mustard's stale. How many times have I told you." "Yes, Madame, Sorry Madame."

"You mustn't leave the mustard out. Oh Philemon! How many times must I tell you?"

"Yes Ma'am. Sorry Ma'am."

The daily humiliation.

The Afrikaners, graves on the farm, will do the dirty work.

The English in Africa.

Everywhere the sun.

Rategan always likes to get "the other side" -- in this case, the men who diligently applied apartheid. The Dark Ones.

To that end he meets with Dr Neil Barnard in a Cape Town Hotel. Tall, broad-face, narrow eyes, black-suited, rangy, son of an apartheid-era education superintendent, brilliant academic, a key backroom engineer in the volatile transition from segregation to majority rule.

Barnard is a figure who has long intrigued Rategan. The youngest head of the feared National Intelligence Service at the age of twenty-nine, twenty-three years later still head of the National Intelligence Service during apartheid's last spasm. Many skeletons in his closets. It was his active intervention, eighty-four meetings with Mandela in jail over four years that built the bridge that Mandela would eventually walk over to Freedom.

After several phone conversations and faxes, he says he wants to meet for minimum of *five* hours. He's read the file on Rategan that shows he is dead serious and highly informed about South Africa.

He says, categorically that he won't do an interview. After getting "burned by the BBC", he doesn't want to "waste my time".

Five hours is good, thinks Rategan. Lap it up. Can't hurt him now.

They meet at a small hotel near Parliament. Rategan imagines it was full of mendacious meetings in the apartheid years.

"Dr Barnard?"

"Niël, please"

A hotel manager greets Barnard familiarly.

On first impressions Barnard is rigid, used to power but awkward without it, ferally suspicious.

He is clearly a proud Afrikaner and rankles at his lack of complete mastery of English, mentioning it twice. Theirs is the discourse of intelligent survivors who know more about each other than either will reveal here.

Rategan manages to stick to his own promise to shut up for a change, and listen, guiding the conversation with short, open-ended questions on a vaguely chronological time-line.

Manners are important. Deference, respect, distance, understanding, even empathy and humour, but with this one, a bull with a dozen eyes, not a false note.

He now consults on security for American clients and for several African heads of state, specialising in jihadist groups across the African continent. It's a growth industry, he says.

And he runs a wild buffalo shooting farm for rich Americans. The easiest of targets, but one missed step, one involuntary tic, and a great fury unleashed.

A stationary Cape Buffalo, it's skull in the crosshairs. That'll be ten thousand US, please.

As the waiter removes their long-chilled coffee tray, Barnard asks Rategan if he minds moving into the smoking area, and he orders some nice crisp white wine. They spend another hour there. Rategan is amused to see him smoke five non-filter cigarettes and swallow three glasses of wine in rapid succession. Behind the narrowed eyes, the man is wired, tense.

His face and manner changes from the taut and circumspect to the flushed and boastful in a matter of minutes. He's now happy to unburden himself before this visitor.

"History will not record my contribution accurately, but that's alright."

Not really.

Barnard stuns Rategan by claiming that several of Mbeki's cabinet ministers are spies, and not only for him, the apartheid spy boss, but for the CIA *and* the KGB.

"We used to know what they were going to do before they put their trousers on in the morning."

He maintains that Mandela would much rather have struck a deal with PW Botha than the somewhat opaque FW de Klerk, and it would have been a better deal. The Barnard option. A ten-year sharing of power. Apartheid ministers and ANC deputy ministers, a rotating wheel of "maximum effectiveness and competency".

Rategan ignores the little bird in his brain reminding him not to express his opinions, but

"There are only two problems with that,"

Barnard's hooded eyes narrow slightly. "Yes?"

"You had extremely bad press... and blood on your hands."

A shutter drops over his eyes.

"And our friends lost their nerve," he says.

There are into a third bottle of a good South African dry white. The air is cloudy with cigarette smoke. This is always the point with South African men, sporting, farming men, when the face is a little red and the tongue a bit loose. Boasting time.

"Your perspective would be critical to the film. Critical. Your Experience. Authority. And interpretation."

Flushed. Sycophancy plus Hubris equals the Hook, set. Amnesty. Maybe not too much to lose. And who will care about a documentary aired in Canada??

"Let me think about doing *this* interview" he says.

Each word falls like a deadweight stone.

He nods once.

Rategan knows he's got him.

FEBRUARY 23

Seven days left. He wakes up at 3:45am. Calls home. Busy, again.

Songbirds in the courtyard.

His field producer's hotel room. A room hit by a whirlwind. Laundry, clean and dirty, files, playback machine, books, newspapers, laptop, VCR, tapes, tapes and tapes, fruit juice, golf clubs, rooibos, kettle, pills, the detritus of his working life, home away from.

Father gasping for last breath. Mother, once the Grace Kelly of Mothers, off the rails. Post-surgery sister, smoking in bed, doing the crossword.

Seven days to go. Running out of time on two interviews. Nelson and Winnie.

He has spoken to someone at the Mandela Foundation called Gloria a number of times. The fourth of fifth time she says

"Yes. You're the Canadian, right."
"Yes, the CBC... Canadian Broadcasting."
"Are you the letter to the new Prime Minister?"

PAUSE. DOUBLE PAUSE.

"No, I'm not the letter to the new Prime Minister."

"Oh." She sounds disappointed. For a moment he is tempted to say, to lie: "Oh... letter to the Prime Minister... yes, yes, of course... The Hon Paul Martin, Dear Sir... congratulations on your election. Hope you continue the great Canadian tradition of supporting democracy in South Africa. Best wishes, Nelson Rolihlahla Mandela."

Rategan's letter to Mandela reaches neither him nor the pit bull Zelda. Like an actor pulling rank, he now knows he has to play the indignation card.

He sends an email directly to John Samuel, the right-hand man, and receives an almost immediate reply, the first decent human response he's had from the whole bunch of them.

Early next morning he phones. Rategan is about to interview his economics analyst, the histrionic Sampie Terreblanche, a Stellenbosch University professor who started out on the far right and is now hurtling off to the far left.

It takes another day of missed calls to connect with John Samuel. He sounds serious, intelligent and genuinely concerned. They arrange a meeting back in Johannesburg.

On his way back to Jo'burg, he hears that Mandela has been spotted in Mauritius. *The News of the World* has a paparazzi shot, fringed by leaves, lounging poolside with Brian May of Queen! A long way from Maputo.

The Nelson Mandela Foundation is, like Mandela's Johannesburg home, palatial and located in the expensive Johannesburg suburb of Houghton Estate. As prestigious companies and consultancies abandoned downtown Johannesburg, they relocated to homes vacated by big white money that had fled, if not to Australia and Canada, further out of the increasingly black city, behind electric wire-topped walls that reach as high as twenty feet.

The building is huge and spacious with fountains, statues and corridors echoing with the brisk cadence of high heels. It's corporate, soulless. A four-foot high statue of Madiba adorns the foyer.

Rategan is ushered into the Walter and Albertina Sisulu boardroom, soon to be joined by the executive assistant to the executive director, Marlene. A woman whose voice he has become familiar with, through his work with the Nelson Mandela Children's Foundation in Canada. She is also Afrikaans, and effusively friendly. They exchange pleasantries about mutual friends in the NMCF. Soon, a small man joins them, with a slightly cultured English accent, John Samuel. Rategan pitches for the interview with Mandela with as much charm and clarity as he can muster -- a pitch that comes from the heart and the head.

There's much note-scribbling on the part of Maeline, the executive assistant to the executive director.

He suddenly visualises Nelson Mandela stretched out on a very well-earned chaise longue at the Mauritius One and Only, blinds over his quarry-damaged eyes, a book by his side, on the phone with Sol Kerzner, the billionaire apartheid-era hotelier.

"Are you alright Madiba? Is there *anything* I can get you?" This from the man who did more than anybody to keep the apartheid "homeland" economies afloat with his luxury resorts. A real gambler.

And Grača, in a sarong, the white-coated waiter bringing drinks, or tea, across the blinding blue terrace.

Samuel is apologising for the run-around Rategan has been getting for the past three months.

"We have extreme documentary fatigue. Mandela is getting frail. But I should be able to get you a 45-minute interview. But not until mid-February or early March (Rategan, as he has pointed out in all his many communications, has to leave for Canada on February 1.)

There are two issues. Firstly, Rategan will have to submit questions in advance, and Mandela will not tell the story he gave to the BBC months before. He feels he has told the whole story, in his book, *No Easy Walk to Freedom*, and with the BBC. He will talk reconciliation, the new South Africa. His legacy.

"Are there any questions he doesn't want to be asked?" Rategan asks.

"No more questions about Aids," Samuel says. And then -- the other shoe.

First control.

Second $.

"And it's our policy here, and you have to understand this is what Madiba prefers, that there is a donation to one of these orphanages."

He taps his finger on a sheet, slides it over.

"It's not a payment to him or the foundation. When you make the contribution, at that time you will be told the name of the institution or school."

The soft thud of third-party charitable corruption? But I must think the best of this man, Rategan thinks. Samuel then asks him for details about his grievances with the way he has been brushed off, misled, and financially probed by various self-appointed gatekeepers. He listens intently and sympathetically, but Rategan feels things have taken a slippery turn.

Insider stroking. The whiff of something foul.

Rategan, like a miner sniffing gas, smells CIA, KPMG, the Canadian liberal establishment, or the CBC, or

Hezbollah, or Mossad, or any one of the massively sleazy big organisations which inevitably come down to a few bright but ruthless people manipulating individuals and other subjects to their dubious ends.

This happens with fame too. Mega-fame like Mandela's is unprecedented. They have no experience of it.

Rategan is the anti-famous. He doesn't really have a prayer.

He is disappointed in Mandela, and himself. Coiled inside, he walks straight-backed out, past the computer desks of softly clicking fingers, through the echoing corridor with its portraits of the struggle, past the towering windows, past the four-feet-tall Madiba, past the smokers at the fountain in the terraced garden, the highway thrumming steel and rubber beyond them.

Rategan has a sinking feeling. But he has options. Bad options, but options.

Rategan is fascinated by Winnie Mandela, as complex a personality as Lady Macbeth. From an angelic Xhosa princess, social worker, solitary prisoner, to a leader as feared as Madame Mao.

Rategan, on the phone in his dishevelled hotel room, the doors and windows open, the sound of children splashing in the pool, fronds bowing in the breeze, is complaining to his researcher that Winnie, who he has met a couple of times, is also avoiding him.

The researcher suggests a surprising go-between: Doc Groenewald. Doc, he tells Rategan, can get Winnie.

"He's an ex-security policeman who had a relationship with her."

Rategan contacts Doc. They meet at a restaurant in a shopping mall. A thirty-something soulful Afrikaner with thinning brown hair, brown eyes, soft brown beard, and the sleepy-soft manner of a baby-faced killer raised on the sjambok[21].

He mumbles a fantastic story about a book he has written. It sounds like a toxic mix of Winnie's revenge -- and a massive Security Branch conspiracy. If Rategan can get the book published overseas, Winnie would favour me. He says he will email it later that day. He does. Rategan receives it but it's too much for his laptop to download.

He calls that night.

"Did you read it yet?"

"Haven't had time. But I will."

"Okay. I'm meeting Winnie at the Hyatt in Rosebank. Ten am. Join us at 10.30.

---

[21] Whip sometimes used to flog kids and labourers (Arikaans)

Informers have been Winnie's bête noire.

After the war, in Paris, they stripped them naked and paraded them through the streets. Tarred and feathered. In South Africa they died under pangas[22] and burning tires.

In the South Africa of his youth, the second of three times Rategan was arrested, it turns out that his name is one of twenty-five given to the security police by a friend. The friend was playing tennis when they came to get him. His brother had been a member of the Communist Party and had been hounded into exile, to the UK. His father had died and his mother was nursing a weak heart. The plainclothesman walked onto the tennis court and took him down to the station in his whites. He placed a telephone in front of him.

"Whose telephone number is 34789?"
"My mother's."
"What will happen if call her and tell her that you have been detained for 180 days."

His gentle friend, believing the news could kill his weak-hearted mother, gives the cop twenty-five names.

On white campuses, one out of three fellow students were totally dependent on state grants, and were often persuaded to inform.

---

[22] Machete-like chopping implements.

In black colleges ninety percent were on government grants. And the alternative was serious poverty, and no university degree. For millions, the fear choice: co-operate or escape.

The trump card of dicatorships everywhere.

What do you do in the townships, when to get some *imali* (money), you say that so and so is ANC?

And so and so who is or is not ANC is taken away and later found dead in a donga[23]? What do you do?

Over the years, as Nelson Mandela survives his 27-year incarceration, Winnie Mandela has relationships with men who then turn around and report to their paymasters, the security police. Talk about sleeping with the enemy, or the devil. Winnie is writing and receiving letters from Mandela, is a key link to the outside world, and to the ANC inside the country, comprehensively banned though it was.

In *The Cry of Winnie Mandela*, author Njabulo Ndebele speculates on the motives of those men. Was there something incredibly arousing about making love to the women loved by the Man? Betrayal of the flesh but not of the heart – but a sickening treachery, for all that.

---

[23] Ditch (Afrikaans)

Mandela didn't see it like that. He told Winnie from the very beginning of his incarceration that she was young, that she must enjoy life as much as possible. He never insisted on fidelity, without directly saying it. Publicly.

All hearts belong to him forever and he'll die inside, anyway, they said.

Poor Winnie, they say, sliding their arms around her, dying inside too.

Rategan sometimes thinks that her madness is her sacrifice to this austere man, screaming as she did to an empty sky.

"He is the people's leader. There is no other. He will return."

Waving her unlit match.

"Together, hand in hand, with our matches and our necklaces, we shall liberate this country"

She is at the Park Hyatt in Rosebank. Rategan sees Doc and her Rategan sees her through the big sad-leaved plants at an outside table. Standing near, two black leather-jacketed plainclothesmen, clearly with Winnie, clearly on the ball, clearly well-dosed with a life's worth of professional paranoia. At 10.30am Rategan joins them, taking a chair near the one plainclothesman, flipping him his plastic CBC ID (no-one ever notices that it's expired).

Rategan has a glass of water which his jacket tips over as he joins them, splashing on to his trousers. Winnie thinks it's hysterical.

"What will your wife think you have been doing with me?" she laughs.

It's a good omen. He remembers the last time he did that at an important job interview 23 years before. He got the job.

There have been some appalling photographs of Winnie in the paper of late, looking like she's on tranks or scotch or both, her hair matted.

But up close she is still beautiful, the skin a lovely soft brown, the eyes dancing with interest, the hand touching Rategan's sleeve often. A security man hands her a cell phone that looks like a miniature electric car. She wanders off into the palm-filled atrium. Returns, apologising.

"The judge got off."

She sits down, looks at me.

"I got him off." She wants me to know.

Across South Africa, Winnie is The Big Interferer. Any controversial case, or arrest, or rally, or tragedy, she's there, Mother of the Nation, salving wounds, attracting the cameras, stirring the pot.

Mandela, the man they named Rolihlahla, "he who shakes the tree" now has a pacifying effect on people. But Winnie has her fist on a branch and shakes it every day.

"They are not going to forget Winnie Mandela."

Rategan tells her he's out doing a documentary film on the life and legacy of Nelson Mandela.

"To tell the story without your input is an injustice to you, and the audience. I could use several available interviews with you, but would rather have you speak now for yourself."

"What available interviews are you using?"

Rategan tells about the interview she gave on the day her husband was sentenced to life, June 14th 1964.

"I shall never lose hope. My people will never lose hope."

"How composed you were, how wedded to the struggle through the Man, how beautiful, young and innocent you looked." Her eyes melt.

He had asked his cameraman Luc for advice as he has, as they say, a way with women.

He thinks for a while and then says: "Compliment her, and then listen to her."

Very good advice. He wishes he had it in his twenties.

The other interview is the one British filmmaker Peter Davis did with her in Brantford when the government sent her into internal exile.

Her eyes narrow. She, like Mandela on Christmas Day, gives Rategan her absolute attention. Scrutiny. Where does this South African from Canada fit into the spectrum of people seeking something from her?

He is aware for a wobbly moment that he is communicating incredibly smoothly with this women, a heroine for one who absolutely subscribes to The Stranglers' "No More Heroes" school of hero worship.

And the word "murderer" passes, as she must have seen it do a hundred times, but he won't miss a beat because this political argument is solved in blood, or the threat of it, and she being one source of this fear.

Winnie: "As you know I don't co-operate with things like this, because I cannot and will not ever talk about the domestic, or personal with him; in fact I will not talk about him at all." It is important to note "him" is said without rancour.

"Also. They always turn out with him the peace-loving humanist and me the violent bitch." She says this last quietly and with effect.

Rategan then tells her his own story, briefly, just so she knows he's from here. He got kicked out in the Seventies. Her eyes wince. "Those were the dark days, my dear", she says, touching his hand again. "Terrible years."

"Oh *I* was alright. You were the one in such danger, terrorised."

She had been in solitary confinement for 18 months, naked the whole time, her menstrual blood caked, cigarettes put into her. She talked to the insects. Rategan tells her he thinks the Eighties were much worse.

"At least the ANC existed, fought back then", she said. "In the '70's we had been wiped from the face of the earth ..."

"Except you," he says.

She laughs.

Rategan tells her how the squatters at the foot of her road in Orlando had bemoaned the lack of money, housing, and jobs.

The ANC and Mandela, she says, are to blame. They have betrayed the poor. Only she still cares.

"That's why I still live here, with them, and not there, with them." Then, as with the I-saved-the-judge comment, letting me know. Those twinkling eyes darkening to coals.

She leans towards Rategan conspiratorially and whispers: "I am the ANC", leaning back regarding Rategan, nodding slightly.

"I am the ANC." The Winnie who brooks no dispute or dilution. (Winnie. Such an inappropriate Victorian slave name. Nomzamo, her first name at birth, would have been better.)

But now, dear Winnie, it doesn't compute. The ANC is a BMW and a posh hotel in Rosebank?

She asks for my name, email, cell phone number, beckoning the other security blade, the one with the date book and phone book, folding it out for Rategan on the table. She says she's happy to do the interview talking "just the way we are talking here."

"But you have to call my lawyer."

She gives him the lawyer's name and number.

Rategan stands up. Eyeing his pants she laughs, easily,

"See, the water's gone!" She thinks it's hysterical.

"Call me" she says.

He leaves, feeling he's got her but knowing it won't be easy. He can't sit with her and not ask about Him, about the murder, the 21 convictions buzzing around her like homing wasps.

Luc is beside him, soundless as silk. "That was good", he says. "do we have her?"
"I have to call her lawyer."

"Uh oh. That's money" he says.
"I know."

Rategan loves what he does. The telling of a story in pictures which will be a viewing choice in a million living rooms of a country like Canada. But the business has become too payola for him. Big political stories are now on the market. The Mandelas, he's told, have a price -- 50 000 US dollars each. He can't stand this, the money part, the grovelling. He can't stand that part of it. He will not make documentaries that involve this any more.

Winnie's lawyer says call another lawyer. He calls the other lawyer. He too angles for money. Rategan gives him the little CBC policy book quote, the slippery slope paragraph. He's not interested, but he says he'll get back to him. Overnight he thinks about this.

He breaks.

He decides to pay her $5 000 out of his own company and not tell the CBC. He calls the lawyer back the next morning and leaves a message to that effect.

The mendacity will wear you down, but as Mandela says: "It is not the number of times I fall, but the number of times I pick myself up" Rategan picks himself up because the documentary demands it.

Later that day, after interviewing the bobbing and weaving mining house mouthpiece Bobby Godsell (who is terribly nice and evasive and reminds Rategan of Barbara Frum's dictum that every interviewee is probably lying), they go out to Winnie's walled-in redoubt in Soweto. The guards say she's not here. Tell her Rategan is here. He goes inside, waves our van in.

They walk, Luc, the soundman Musa and he into the front door past a vast dining room crammed with gifts of every description from foreign dignitaries, parliaments, sultans, presidents, moguls, organisations.

To the left are two security men on computers. They are waved into an overwrought living room, packed with colour, gifts, kitschy statuary, an overall sense, if not the reality, of velvet paintings.

After ten minutes, Winnie and her daughter Zindzi descend into the adjoining dining room. They both float, dressed in diaphonous fabrics. Zindzi has a riot of tiny light golden ringlets. Winnie greets Rategan like a long-lost comrade, hugging him tightly for seconds on each side and planting a big kiss on his mouth.

She smells like baby powder. He is physically grateful for the deep softness of her body. He feels he is being comforted by Mother Africa herself, and he is briefly undone. Come unto me all ye wretched of this racist earth and I will fill you with love, unity… and rebellion. They talk. Musa and Luc are a little gobsmacked.

She asks him again exactly what he would ask her, on camera. He goes over the same territory.

He remembers during the worst daysof apartheid, her lashing out at a security policemen on a highway, on TV. He'd ask her about her fury.

"First we had stones. Then we had Molotovs. Then we had AK-47s."

They talk for half an hour. Rategan tells her the story of when he'd driven past Pretoria Central and sung Happy Birthday to her after his first arrest for being a white interloper in a black church. The fact that she must have heard thousands of these stories doesn't lessen the intensity of how she receives it. She acknowledges, particularly when Rategan mentions his companion's name that night, Jeanette. When Zindzi asks if it is the Jeannette from Norwood, Winnie and Rategan both refer to the bomb that blew her up in Lubango, northern Angola.

It is a convivial, positive meeting, until … until he says he will (waving an imaginary match) ask her about the famous necklacing speech, in which she reportedly said: "With our boxes of matches and our necklaces we will liberate this country."

A cloud covers her brow, eyes narrowing. Rategan blathers on about how most Canadians couldn't imagine having to go that far.

Zindzi then says there would have to be some kind of approval of the final script. Rategan knows it's slipping away but presses on.

"I am absolutely happy to let you see the script but I have to tell you that I can only guarantee listening to your objections."

And then he adds, from Journalism Ethics 101: "I have to tell you, in my case, that neither God, nor Nelson nor Winnie Mandela, nor the KGB nor the CIA nor David Beckham himself can tell me what I can or cannot say as an objective documentary filmmaker."
There is the brief, stiff silence the follows one hard-ass bumping into another.

Winnie smiles slightly; Zindzi says: "And David Beckham, they say, is more popular than Jesus."
All laugh.

She says she will do the interview. Call the first lawyer.

Rategan waits for an hour. He calls the lawyer. He is in Lesotho. He says he will see Rategan in his chambers the day after tomorrow.

Rategan misses his family. It's been more than two months on the road.

With three days to go, he is told he has Nelson; Winnie says he has her -- he just needs to arrange a meeting with the man who is to compose the music for the documentary, who he hired two months earlier.

He goes to see Winnie's lawyer. A terse man with a runaway train as a client.

After listening inscrutably to Rategan's pitch he offers him a grape. He is wearing a cerise shirt with a high white collar that would make Don Cherry envious. In a world-weary way he says he has instructed Winnie not to grant any interviews until her appeal, two months hence, against embezzlement charges. He blathers on like lawyers everywhere about his client's innocence. Rategan points out that the case is not touched on in the film. Mendacity the Mosquito buzzes deafeningly in the room. Through the window behind him is the courthouse where a death squad killer in another case is walking free.

In the passageway Mandela's lawyer appears, briefly. Winnie's lawyer works at Nelson lawyer's firm. Hmm.

Rategan senses there is a gag order on Winnie, part of the divorce settlement.

"Now they try her in magistrate's court, before a stupid white magistrate, an Afrikaner, and a white jury. Just like the old days."

Suddenly Don Cherry and his grape is a spitting cobra.

Rategan is fatigued, down for the count.

He wants to hug his children. He is impeccably warm and polite. As he leaves the lawyer says. "My client is desirous of doing an interview with you. In June, after the appeal. She has also suggested that you should be the filmmaker to make her story. She has taken to you, it seems. Please send us a proposal on doing her film, and we will workshop it."

Workshop it. My God.

His musician/composer calls in a prima donna-like froth from Cape Town. Recently nominated for an Oscar, he is drowning in offers and doesn't think he can give Rategan's film the "attention it deserves". Rategan is furious but contains it. He shuts him off with an impossibly tight goodbye, like the woman on the Weakest Link.

His sister has received a fax from John Samuel regrettably turning down his request to interview Mr Mandela, who is swamped.

In a day he has lost Madiba, Winnie and his composer.

This documentary is proving to be whiplash. Within 24 hours, Winnie has called him and now promised an interview the day before we leave: he has found a musician who turns out to be an award-winner, and the fax from the Mandela Foundation is a response to the request Rategan faxed them on December 9, weeks before his meeting with John Samuel and his promise of an interview in mid- or late February.

Twenty-four hours later. He has spent the whole day in his hotel room waiting for the promised call from Winnie, but he has used the time well. Knowing every image and syllable at his disposal, and having the story down cold anyway, he structures the two-hour film. As he finishes it he gazes at the print-out.

It will serve the Canadian people: an incredible, true story of great political and human courage.

One for the ages.

In the end he gets neither an exclusive with Nelson or Winnie. He uses clips of Mandela from the BBC, and clips from Winnie where he can find them.

The story that propelled him out of South Africa, completely changed the course of his life 32 years before, has been told, for millions. It's the best he can do.

The documentary "Madiba: The Life and Times of Nelson Mandela" is described by Canada's leading TV critic as the best biography documentary ever aired on the CBC.

In a friend's house in Johannesburg Mandela views the documentary. "That's the best one" he tells Rategan's friend.

To this day, every Mandela Day in South Africa, the documentary is re-aired. For CBC it is their best-selling biography documentary.

And Rategan knows that in the audience, the odd child gets it.

Watches, and understands.

-30-

THE DOCUMENTARIES:

Madiba: The Life and Times of Nelson Mandela.

John Doyle "The best Life and Times ever" https://www.theglobeandmail.com/arts/ nelson-mandelas-many-faces/article1133431/Globe and Mail.

Gemini Award: best music.
Gemini Nomination: Best Biography program.

https://cogentbenger.com/documentaries/
mandela-life-and-times/